CREATION'S STORY

Creation's Story

Robert W. Cargill

JOHN RITCHIE LTD
CHRISTIAN PUBLICATIONS

40 Beansburn, Kilmarnock, Scotland

ISBN-13: 978 1 904064 61 9
ISBN-10: 1 904064 61 2

www.ritchiechristianmedia.co.uk

Front Cover: Sunset glow on the Matterhorn, Swiss Alps (see p.63)
Back Cover: Atlantic surf on Scottish beach, with arctic tern (see p.124)
(photographs by the author)

Typeset by John Ritchie Ltd., Kilmarnock
Printed by Bell & Bain Ltd., Glasgow

"The heavens declare the glory of God;
and the firmament sheweth His handiwork.
Day unto day uttereth speech
and night unto night sheweth knowledge.
There is no speech nor language where
their voice is not heard."

(Ps 19.1-3)

"Thou art worthy, O Lord, to receive glory
and honour and power:
for Thou hast created all things,
and for Thy pleasure they are and were created."

(Rev 4.11)

Contents

Foreword

Atheism appears to be more fashionable than ever. It is, of course, not at all new. The "fool who has said in his heart, 'There is no God' " (Ps 13.1) has been around for millennia. This is despite the clear evidence spoken of by the Psalmist that "The heavens declare the glory of God; and the firmament sheweth His handywork" (Ps 19.1). And this declaration, he explains, is given in a way that can be understood by all whatever their native language.

Of course, for some, the theory of Evolution is a prop to their unbelief. But their apparent confidence that God is redundant is not well placed. A careful study of the world around us should lead to the conclusion not only that there is a God who made it all but also that His wisdom and glory are therein displayed. Several books have been written of late that ought to give pause to those who dismiss this evidence. Some of these are referred to in the bibliography that Bert Cargill has appended to this book. This volume is a worthy complement to them.

It is worth remembering that long before Darwin was born the conclusion of Scripture is that "the invisible things of Him from the creation of the world are clearly seen, being understood by the things that are made, even His eternal power and Godhead; so that they are without excuse" (Rom 1.20).

The technical and scientific arguments involved in debates about the universe and about life are complex. It is valuable to have them put in simple – but not simplistic – terms by someone with expertise in several of the key subjects. These chapters should give sufficient insight for believers without any specialized knowledge to assure them that it is not contrary to reason to believe that "In the beginning God created the heaven and the earth" (Gen 1.1) and that "All things were made by Him and without Him was not anything made that was made" (Jn 1.3). The latter of these quotations is a clear statement of Special Creation as the explanation for all that surrounds us.

A particular pleasure in this book is that all the way through it seeks to draw spiritual lessons for our benefit. While dealing with science it is firmly based on the Scriptures and has the grand objective of drawing attention to the glory of God. It is a pleasure to commend it.

W S Stevely
Ayr
Sept 2008

Introduction

The different chapters of this book first appeared in monthly issues of the *Believer's Magazine* during 2007 and 2008. In response to requests to make the material available in a more permanent form, these have been collated here after light editing for the benefit of a wider readership. The chapters are now arranged in four coherent parts as you can see on the 'Contents' page.

The motive behind both this and the original articles is to show how all and any parts of the material universe, large and small, animate and inanimate, declare the wisdom and power of their great Creator and bear witness to Him. By retelling and rereading the great and fascinating story of creation we are more able to glorify Him enthusiastically for what He has done, for what only He could do. We echo the words of David's Psalm: "All Thy works shall praise Thee, O LORD; and all Thy saints shall bless Thee" (Ps 145.10).

This is not another book which sets out to 'disprove' evolution or to 'prove' creation. We are starting from the fundamental statement that "In the beginning God created the heavens and the earth" (Gen 1.1), and that "without Him (the Lord Jesus Christ) was not anything made that was made" (Jn 1.3). We are really taking for granted that readers already believe that the Bible is the Word of God and therefore it is accurate, authoritative, and true from beginning to end.

However, if some of my readers do have genuine doubts or sincere questions about evolution and/or creation please read on with an open mind. Different viewpoints are a matter of individual choice for reasons best known to the individual. This is not a scientific book, nor does it require much knowledge of science to grasp its message. As for the science, I can only assure you that I have found that the observed and established facts of science totally harmonise with the revelation of Scripture. After the major part of a lifetime involved with teaching and scientific research, in chemistry to be precise, I and many others have found that creation-based interpretations of the facts make more sense than do evolution-based ones. Some of the following chapters will show you this. The sad situation is that most people want, indeed demand evolution-based explanations and nothing else. Therefore such explanations are generally propagated without allowing a serious consideration of any alternative, and they are accepted blindly and uncritically. You owe it to yourself to consider this.

I want to record my thanks to John Grant, editor of the *Believer's Magazine,* for his encouragement to do the original writing and to keep it going, to many readers of that magazine who have expressed their interest and appreciation of the material in different ways, to Bill Stevely for writing the Foreword, to the directors and staff of John Ritchie Ltd for their help and cooperation in supporting this project, and last but not least to my wife Isobel for her patience and understanding during many hours at the computer.

Bert Cargill
St Monans
Scotland
Sept 2008

PART 1

AN OVERVIEW – FROM BEGINNING TO END

In which we consider –

what the Bible teaches us about our Creator;

what we are told about the beginning

of creation and its end;

who it is that sustains it and how it all keeps going;

why everything is becoming more disordered as time passes.

CHAPTER 1

The Creator's Glory

Creation's story reveals the great Creator's glory. You can see it wherever you look. Look up into the night sky studded with countless stars, look down into the ocean depths full of amazing life forms, look out across a spreading landscape or seascape or over a cottage garden, be stirred by a golden sunset or a rose tinted dawn. Take a telescope and look further, take a microscope and look closer, take a textbook and study deeper, take a journey and go farther, take time and listen and look and touch and breathe in slowly. What happens? Your senses respond. Your mind and heart are stirred. You can find that as in another structure which God designed, "Everything saith, Glory" (Ps 29.9, RV).

Explore it as much as you can, enjoy it, admire it, appreciate it, try to understand it. And then from it all appreciate Him who created you too - His masterpiece. Then bow your heart and give Him all the glory.

Glory Revealed
The glory of God has been revealed in many ways, indeed it is revealed in all His works and ways. The Holy Scriptures are themselves a treasure-house of glory. The more we search, humbly and diligently, the more we will find to move our hearts in adoration and worship. The more too we will absorb that glory and reflect it to others (2 Cor 3.18). Also we see the glory of God shining in the face of Jesus Christ our Saviour (4.6). And the great plan of redemption worked out at Calvary is a glorious

one, so much so that those who have benefited from it will be to the glory of His grace for ever (Eph 1.6).

These are "joys unspeakable and full of glory" (1 Pet 1.8). They thrill our souls. But sometimes we give less attention than we should to another realm in which the glory of God is revealed, to His amazing work in Creation which reveals His surpassing wisdom and almighty power.

All of the material, physical universe, 'all creatures great and small', from the largest mammal to the smallest insect or bacterium, from the huge planets in the solar system to the tiny electrons in the atom - they have all come from the hand of God, created and upheld by the Word of His power. To overlook this is to miss something important. "The things that are made" are an eloquent testimony to God, revealing "His eternal power and Godhead" (Rom 1.20).

Evolution Theory
To give to the Lord our God the glory due to His name is one of the fundamental reasons for our very existence. Every true believer delights to do this at all times and for all reasons, and it will be our blessed occupation for all eternity. However, one of Satan's great objectives is to rob God of that glory, and to do so by whatever means he can.

One of the most successful methods by which God's greatness and glory have been denied is through the propagation of the theory of evolution. It is indoctrinated into every level of education in every developed country of the world. The mass media assume it at every turn. The scientific press is supposed to be fair and neutral, but sections of it continue a relentless crusade against "creationism" for no other reason than that it "cannot be accepted"! Opposition to the idea of evolution is not permitted, rather ridiculed. But the reason for its popularity is not its objective truth, but rather the strong bias that God is not wanted.

15

It is not the case that evolution has disproved the existence of God, although many say so. It is a mindset of atheism which has led to evolution, not evolution that leads to atheism. Unwillingness to face the implications of accountability to God has made evolution very desirable. It provides an excuse (which is presented as a scientific reason) to evade the obvious and the logical - that the universe and everything in it was created, bearing the clear evidence of design and purpose. This evidence is in fact the evidence of the wisdom and the power of the almighty God.

Evolution is a theory, a proposed explanation for the origin and the development of everything biological, and indeed more besides. Charles Darwin's book, *The Origin of the Species*, published in 1859, gave it a huge impetus. Since then, the theory has undergone many changes and revisions, as often happens to theories in science, but some of the revisions are mutually contradictory. Evolution is certainly not a fact, in spite of what is often stated.

Observations and facts of science have been arranged around the theory of evolution and some have been selected to support it. But these observations and facts can be explained much better by the theory (or if you prefer, the doctrine) of creation. The creation account of origins does not violate any established fact or law of science. Evolution theory does, however, and therefore it is not good science. It cannot be a sound scientific theory, for it is contradicted by several of these laws, e.g. thermodynamics (energy), biogenesis (life), and information science, to mention a few which we will explore later.

Creation

The title Creator is used relatively few times in both Old and New Testaments. It is worth checking these with a concordance. But the doctrine of creation pervades the whole Bible from literally the first verse to well through the last book. The key passages to study in the New Testament are

John 1.1-5; Romans 1.19-25; 8.18-25; Colossians 1.14-19; Hebrews 1.1-4,10-12; and 2 Peter 3.3-13. The main points are these:

- The original source and origin of everything is God, who Himself is uncreated and eternal.
- The power of God to create was manifest in His spoken word.
- All life comes from God, simple and complex, animal and vegetable, physical and spiritual, present and eternal.
- The Son of God is both the designer and maker of everything in the whole universe. It was created by Him and for Him. He also upholds or maintains it in all its functions
- The present state of the material world and the living things it contains has been modified from its original state because of the sin of our first parents in Eden. It is in fact steadily deteriorating and losing some of its splendour - at a global level even now this is being accelerated by man's mismanagement of his environment.
- The material creation is not permanent. In God's time it will be totally destroyed, after it has served its purpose, when God's day of grace is followed by the day of judgement in its final form.
- There will eventually be a new heaven and a new earth in which righteousness will dwell for ever.

Our Creator
God is our strong Redeemer, our blessed Saviour, our loving heavenly Father. He is also our faithful Creator. To Him we commit the keeping of our souls (1 Pet 4.19).

It is He who made us, and not we ourselves (Ps 100.3). All that we are physically and mentally, our fearfully and wonderfully made bodies and our amazingly complex and efficient minds, carry the imprint of a divine hand. It is important to value them, use them properly and care for them - indeed to glorify Him in our bodies (1 Cor 6.20). And when advancing age or disease take their toll we can confidently commit their care to Him who remembers that we are dust (Ps 103.14), frail and mortal, yet crafted by His skill.

God's power in the universe is immense - unmeasurable. There is no searching of His understanding. Nothing fails or gets out of the place of His arrangement: "behold who hath created these things ... not one faileth" (Isa 40.26). He numbers and names the stars, but He also numbers the hairs of our heads and sees when the sparrow falls to the ground. He is almighty over all yet so tender to each one of us, infinite and eternal, but close and personal to those who trust in Him.

Solomon's advice was to remember our Creator in the days of our youth (Eccl 12.1). This gives to life a sure foundation, and when youth has passed, even long past, this truth is as relevant as ever. He made us. He saves us. He keeps us. He will never leave us. Even the dust of believers' bodies in the grave is in His custody until the day of resurrection.

In this book, some aspects of creation will be explored and described in such a way as to give to God the glory due to His Name. Believers in Christ can also be confident that notwithstanding the heavy bombardment which continues to come from the evolution camp, the foundation of the Lord stands sure. His Word is totally trustworthy, and a belief in the literal Bible account of origins is totally sustainable.

CHAPTER 2

The Beginning:
"the Foundation of the World"

A unique and majestic statement makes up the first verse of our Bibles. In a few words is contained the answer to a fundamental question before it was even asked. Down the ages many have wondered: "Where did everything come from?" "What was the beginning of it all?" Genesis 1.1 tells us!

"In the beginning, God created …" He is the first cause and origin of everything. Accepting this statement by faith (Heb 11.3) is the most reasonable thing to do. It matches everyday experience that every single thing has a maker, a designer, an author, a cause, a creator. This surely includes the marvellous, intricate, beautiful natural world. But evolution theory says it does not. This is not reasonable or logical, and it is not truly scientific either, in spite of loud claims that it is. Real science is based upon actual observation and measurement, and *nothing* has ever been observed happening without a cause, or evolving out of chaos, or coming from nothing.

Every painting has its artist, every structure its architect and builder, every book its author. Due credit and even glory are properly given to the creators of works of merit and beauty which people appreciate. Now we believe that "without Him was not anything made that was made" (John 1.3). From the tiniest sub-atomic particle to the greatest galaxy, from the smallest single flower and its pollen grain to the working arrangement of bees in a hive or ants in a colony or deer in a herd, we admire beauty and complexity. In our admiration we give glory to their great Creator. Evolution theory denies Him that glory, indeed denies that He exists. Why? because atheism is its starting point, not its conclusion. It is what so many people want to believe.

But what do we believe, particularly about when and how and why everything began? We are clearly told why: "*for Thy pleasure they are and were created*" (Rev 4.11). As to when and how, it is important to give proper weight and meaning to the statements of Genesis 1, and at the same time not to import into that chapter what is not there.

No Dates
We are *not* told when "the beginning" was, when the earth was created, or when Adam was made. No dates are given in the text of Genesis 1. Some calculations have been made, but all these calculations contain certain assumptions which are probably not valid.

Evolutionists claim that the earth was formed about 4.5 thousand million years ago. Their calculation is based upon the measured rate of radioactive processes in certain rocks. The calculation contains two major assumptions:
  (1) the rate has not changed over vast periods of time and in extremely variable conditions;
  (2) none of the elements produced by these radioactive processes were in the rocks to begin with.
Both of these assumptions are probably not correct for good scientific reasons. So, although that figure is often quoted, it is not a reliable fact. There are other scientific methods to measure the age of the earth, and they come up with much smaller numbers, some less than 10,000 years [1]. These are neglected, in fact rejected, just because they do not fit the requirements of evolution theory and its interpretation of the fossil record.

Archbishop Usher in 1664 calculated that Adam was created in 4004 BC. His calculation used genealogical lists in the Old Testament, working back from more recent dates. This method also contains assumptions which might be quite wrong, e.g., that the genealogical lists have no missing generations, which sometimes they have. Indeed, using similar methods others have arrived at dates which range from 6984 to 3616 BC [2]. This just means that we cannot be sure of exactly when Adam was created, or when the world began. The date 4004 BC does appear in the margin or column notes of many Bibles, but remember it does *not* exist in the inspired text and should not be taken as a serious fact!

No Gaps

The narrative of Genesis 1 is a continuous one. To introduce breaks or gaps is to force an idea which is not in the text. The case for the once popular "Gap Theory", which inserts "geological ages" between verses 1 and 2, is at best extremely weak indeed, based on a possible meaning of two words. It also creates more problems than it tries to solve, and at worst it misrepresents God and compromises the truth. Again, its appearance in margin or footnotes in certain editions of the Bible has influenced many readers. But it too is *not* in the inspired text!

The Gap Theory was a well-meaning but misguided attempt to deal with attacks being made in the nineteenth century by "science" on the veracity of Genesis 1. It was claimed that millions of years of "geological time" were required for the earth and its strata to be formed, complete with their fossils. A scientist, Georges Cuvier of Paris, first proposed that repeated catastrophic floods produced fossils, and that these took place in prehistoric ages long before Adam. In the UK this idea was actively promoted by the theologian Thomas Chalmers, and then followed by several well known Bible teachers. They claimed that an "original creation" described in Genesis 1.1 was laid waste in judgement by God, its "pre-Adamic creatures" fossilised, then ages later God "remade" the earth as described in the rest of Genesis 1. Many who were concerned about the threat of science to Scripture thought that things "harmonised" by putting this gap between two verses.

In fact they didn't harmonise, and real problems exist with it! The clear teaching of Scripture is this:
• Adam was the first man, so there were no people before him on any kind of earth;
• It was Adam's sin which brought death into the world, so if any "pre-Adamic creatures" did exist their death to produce fossilised remains is not explainable.
• God pronounced all His creation "very good"- not a very apt description if its rocks contained the evidence of death, destruction and judgement.

The creation described in Genesis 1 was perfect, not a reconstruction of a something that 'became' without form and void.

As we shall see later, the best and most consistent explanation of fossils, strata, and geological phenomena is provided from the effects of the great flood in the days of Noah. This is a well documented event with profound results on mankind and his environment, not a tenuous theory with imaginary causes or effects of which there is no evidence in the divine revelation.

No Defects
All God's works are perfect. When He made everything as recorded in Genesis 1 He made it all perfect at the first attempt. It was not, as some would teach, that God started the process off, then used evolution to advance and complete it. This "theistic evolution" is another serious compromise which insults God and His Word, for evolution is an extremely wasteful and callous process, involving many life forms which did not survive. God is never wasteful or callous of any of His creatures.

Man needs many attempts at achieving an objective, has to experiment and improve on earlier versions, but not God. In the beginning God made every creature without defect, male and female, ready to reproduce and take their place in a benign and unspoilt earth. It was also a mature creation, which would *appear to be* a certain age, e.g., Adam might have looked like a 30(?)-year old man; trees bearing ripened fruit might contain 20(?) annual growth rings whereas they were created the day before; distant stars appearing to be very old (to allow time for their light to travel through space) having been created with their light rays already reaching earth.

The defects and deficiencies so prevalent now are the result of the Fall. Disease and death face us daily. The animal and vegetable kingdoms contain many evidences of decay and degeneration. Many species have become extinct, while many subspecies have changed and developed in response to environmental pressures and conditions. The present world is vastly different from how it left the hand of God. It has degenerated into something inferior, *not* evolved into something better.

In conclusion then, when was the beginning? Three things to note –

- God Himself has no beginning (John 1.1). He is from everlasting to everlasting. We time-bound people find that difficult to comprehend, but it is true nonetheless. His name is Jehovah – the ever existing One.
- The Genesis 1.1 beginning may be classified as "the foundation of the world". Its date is unknown, nor does it really matter. Just rejoice that we were chosen in Christ before that.
- Adam's life began unlike ours in fully developed manhood, as did Eve's shortly after. How long ago that was cannot be determined precisely, but it would be in keeping with Biblical

revelation and established fact to say it was less than 10,000 years ago.

---

1. More details in *And God Said*; F Abou-Rahme, Ch. 9
2. Young's Analytical Concordance: "creation"

CHAPTER 3

The End: "All These Things Dissolved"

The disciples asked the Lord Jesus one day, "When shall these things be? And what ... of the end of the world?" (Matt 24.3). Such questions about the end have often been asked, as have the questions about the beginning which we considered in the last chapter.

Many attempts have been made to provide answers, and even give dates for the end, some based on ingenious calculations which only their exponents can follow, others by attempting to extract from history the fulfilment of specific prophesies of Scripture, even others from superstition! But our Lord's words are apposite: "it is not for you to know the times or the seasons ... but ye shall be witnesses unto me." (Acts 1.7-8). Curiosity about future times must not turn us from present responsibility. It is not that God has not told us about the future. Much has been told us, particularly that the Lord is coming soon. But *when*, we do not know! We do know, however, that the Rapture will initiate events to take place on earth and in heaven, as revealed in the Scriptures, before the end does come.

This earth is the platform (or stage) upon which the great drama of redemption is being worked out. The effects of that wonderful work will be everlasting, but the earth on which it happened is not everlasting. We are now going to look at what will happen to the present creation, how it will end.

2 Peter 3 declares that there are *three different "heavens and earth":*

(1) "the heavens *were of old,* and the earth" (v.5), the "world that then was". It was overflowed by the waters of the great flood of Genesis 7.

(2) "the heavens and the earth, *which are now*" (v.7). This is reserved unto fire in the day of judgement which is yet future.

(3) *"new* heavens and a *new* earth wherein dwelleth righteousness" (v.13), which John also saw in his great vision (Rev 21.1); when the former things had passed away and there is an eternal state of blessedness.

"The heavens and the earth" in this context is the total environment made for man. To show how this present "heaven and earth" will end, three instructive phrases are used in the New Testament:
• everything will be *"delivered up"*
• they will be *"folded up"*
• they will be *"burned up"*.

Delivered up

1 Corinthians 15.24 tells us of *"the end,* when He shall have *delivered up* the kingdom to God, even the Father; when He shall have put down all rule and all authority and power." What is described here is the ultimate and full victory of our Lord Jesus over every enemy which has invaded this world, including the "last" one, death (v.26). This earth, since man's fall in Eden, has been the scene of much rebellion against God, of the relentless struggle of evil against good, of wars and strife, of centuries of sadness and sorrow for mankind. But also on this earth, God's Son appeared to put away sin by the sacrifice of Himself, and to deliver from Satan's power all those who trust in Him. That work at Calvary is the guarantee of ultimate liberty and eternal triumph for the redeemed.

So before the present heaven and earth reach the end of their appointed time and purpose, there has to be the full and final overthrow of every enemy and the subjugation of every rebel force. Christ will do that, via the great battle of Armageddon in the land of Israel, and then around a thousand years later, the final battle of all which concludes with the devil cast into the lake of fire (Rev 20.10). All His enemies will be put under His feet. In "righteousness He will judge and make war" (Rev 19.11). Our blessed Lord will deliver up to God the Father a fully completed and perfected work of grace and government on this earth where it began.

Folded up

Among the superior glories of the Son of God described in Hebrews 1 is His creatorial power, vv.10-12. In the beginning He laid the foundation of the earth. We marvel again at "the works of His hands". From our view-point they seem so permanent. Even Scripture speaks of "the everlasting hills" (Gen 49.26). But they are not permanent. "They shall perish; ... wax old; Thou shalt *fold them up*, and they shall be changed."

The figure is that of a garment which has served its purpose, but is already showing signs of wear and tear. That is what we see all around us, for example in the diminishing of the earth's resources as raw materials are used up, as sea and land become plundered and exhausted of food supplies, and energy resources dwindle. This planet has supported man and countless other life forms for several millennia, but the task is getting harder. The "garment" is getting thinner and is stretching to near breaking point.

What will happen next? Our Lord Jesus will fold it up – not allow it to go into tatters. Just like an old worn coat, it will be folded away and replaced with a new one. He is in control, so that when the appropriate time comes, He will change this present environment altogether and introduce a better one which will not grow old. But He will not change. He remains the person He has ever been. He will outlast the work of His hands. "Thou art the same, and Thy years fail not" – "the same, yesterday, and today, and for ever" (Heb 13.8).

Burned up

The words of 2 Peter 3 present a different picture. The context is about God keeping His promises, although the ungodly do not think so. They think that things just go on and on and on as usual. The chapter points out how God does interrupt history, in a drastic way, first with a great flood, and next with a great fire. His time scale is different from man's, however. He is longsuffering and He never sends judgement without first sending mercy and opportunity to be saved.

The present world, we are told, is reserved unto fire. "The earth also and the works that are therein shall be *burned up*". The graphic words of vv.10-11 present a scene of total destruction, even annihilation – "pass away with a great noise; elements melt with fervent heat; all things dissolved".

Words such as these have been used about catastrophic events which this world has already witnessed, and which may provide a clue to the fulfilment of 2 Peter 3. The terrible destructive force of nuclear explosions is well known. In these, small amounts of matter are converted into energy almost instantaneously, with extremely devastating effects. Nuclear fission, (as in the atomic bomb or in a reactor for production of electricity) and nuclear fusion (as in the hydrogen bomb) are processes which release truly immense amounts of energy. This is a consequence of the way that God designed the atom.

Atoms are composed of a nucleus containing protons and neutrons with energy fields to keep them in place, and electrons which move very fast around the nucleus also in their energy fields. But by far the biggest part of every atom is empty space between the nucleus and the moving electrons. So when an atom collapses, these vast amounts of energy are released, and where there was solid matter, there is just empty space, nothing. Einstein's equation shows how much energy can be obtained from matter, and matter (the stuff of the universe) can be thought of as a form of energy or power.

Now this agrees with the fact that all things were created and are upheld "by the word of His power". That power is there for His purposes of providence or government. At the appropriate time that power will be released in the disintegration of the earth and everything in it. That same eternal power will then rebuild a new and better world altogether.

It is solemn to realise that everything around us, made up of atoms, already contains within it the means and mechanism of its destruction. The world of Genesis 6 was like that too - the waters of the flood had been stored in a huge vapour canopy above the earth and fountains deep beneath, ready and waiting for God to use to flood the earth in judgment. Another example of this may be the existence of earth's greatest rift valley up through North Africa all the way to the Jordan valley, where we are told that profound geological changes will one day occur to split the mount of Olives in two and bring a sea of waters to Jerusalem (Zech 14.4-8). God who knows the end from the beginning has everything in place for His purpose long before it is required.

Delivered up, folded up, or *burned up* – this world will one day reach the end of its appointed purpose. But Christ and His kingdom are eternal, and His people will share His glory "throughout all ages, *world without end*, Amen" (Eph 3.21).

CHAPTER 4

A "Groaning Creation"

So far we have considered how God in the beginning "laid the foundations of the earth" (Ps 104.5), and in wisdom made all the manifold works it contains (v.24). We have also seen from Scripture that in a future day He will bring about the end of it all, indeed the disappearance of it all, after it has served its purpose.

But what is happening just now in the created realm in which we live and of which we form a part? Is it simply proceeding under its own momentum, like an old fashioned rail-truck being shunted until it slows down to a stop, or a sledge speeding down a snowy hillside until it crashes? Or are we whirling through space on planet earth held by invisible forces which will never be changed? No; none of these views is correct!

Actually two things are happening at the same time, according to the Scriptures. One is that the Lord Jesus Christ is "upholding all things by the word of His power" (Heb 1.3). The One who created all things is in control of them, keeping them going according to His wisdom and power. There will be no cosmic collision or unplanned collapse of our world. In His great love He cares for mankind, so that before this world perishes and does vanish away, His grace has planned and provided a future in a far better world for all who trust in Him.

The other thing that is happening is that this universe is naturally decaying and steadily deteriorating. We can see this all around us on planet earth, the part of the universe we know best. The entrance of sin, "by one man" (Rom 5.12), has altered everything. The ground has been cursed and "the whole creation now groans and travails in pain until now", says Romans 8.22. It is vastly different from Eden.

We will look at this decay and degeneration first, then in our next chapter see how everything is held by a hand that never loses control.

Running down

The universe has been likened to a huge clock which was wound up in the beginning, and is slowly ticking away with ever less of the spring reserve left available. There is some truth in this picture, sometimes used in popular science but without acknowledging the divine hand which 'made the clock', 'wound the spring', and can advance it or retard it!

We sometimes hear that the stars are 'burning out'. For us the best example is the sun upon which physical life on earth depends. The sun is a gigantic star which is slowly being consumed as its material mass is turned into light and heat and other forms of radiation by the process of nuclear fusion. Its hydrogen atoms are being converted into helium atoms with the release of huge amounts of energy. From the rate at which this is happening, it has been calculated how many millions of years it will be until it 'burns out'. The change in the sun's radiation is not noticeable during centuries of time, but if it ever stopped shining, even for a few days on end, life on planet earth would quickly become extinct. Our God continues to make it rise on the evil and on the good (Matt 5.45). But it is a fact that its energy is being expended and the amount left is decreasing.

Irreversible run down can be seen on earth also. Mountains and hills are slowly eroding by the forces of wind and rain, frost and snow, cold and heat. Rivers are becoming more silted as run-off from adjacent land carries material with it. The seas are becoming more salty. The atmosphere is also changing as lighter gases escape through the stratosphere and others are added. Everywhere chemical reactions are taking place to produce materials which are less useful and with less energy in them than the starting materials. All of this adds up to a picture of "change and decay" on earth, even before we start to take account of what is happening in the living systems on earth, and also what effects man has had upon the planet.

"The Bondage of Corruption"

When we look into the plant and animal kingdoms the effects are just as evident. The result of the curse, the "thorns and thistles", has only got worse down the years. Food crops have to compete more and more with weeds old and new. Farming and gardening are in a constant battle with unwanted growth. Whilst it is true that weeds are only "plants growing in the wrong place", the places where they thrive seem to be always where crops are intended to grow. Added to the problem of weeds is the incidence of diseases, parasites, fungi, and insect defoliants (e.g., weevils and locusts). Chemicals have been applied with some success to control weeds, diseases and pests, but side effects are a concern. For "the desert to blossom as the rose" requires the removal of the curse, not huge irrigation schemes or the application of chemistry! The groaning creation can be seen all around the countryside.

On every continent can also be seen "nature red in tooth and claw". Predators of all sizes devour prey of every description, among the animals on the land, the birds of the air, the fish of the sea, and the insects everywhere. The death of one species enables the survival of another. This is the way of today's world. The effects of the curse can be heard in the howl of the wolf, the roar of the lion, the hoot of the owl, the hiss of the snake, the wing beat of the mosquito, and the groans of their prey. In the future when Christ reigns, it will be different: "they shall not hurt nor destroy in all my holy mountain" (Isa 65.25); but just now "sin reigns unto death" (Rom 5.21).

As for ourselves, when the vigour of youth declines and the limitations of old age increase, the groaning is often literal and audible. Accidents or mishaps may precipitate these groans at any stage in life. Aches and pains appear, diseases and illnesses happen: "we ourselves groan within ourselves, waiting for the redemption of the body" (Rom 8.23). This redemption is a wonderful prospect, but meantime we are thankful for pain killers and a host of other medicines. These bodies of humiliation (Phil 3.21) are part of the legacy of the Fall, and are not immune from its effects. But it will be different when Christ comes – we will have a body like His, delivered fully and finally from all the effects of sin. Then in the glorious liberty of the children of God, we, and the creature also, shall be delivered from the bondage of corruption (Rom 8.21). We shall go out with joy, be led forth with peace; the mountains and the hills shall sing in harmony with us, and the trees shall clap their hands (Isa 55.12).

Man's Stewardship
The natural run down of earth and its systems has been greatly accelerated by man's activities, increasingly so as the centuries pass. God committed to man the care and use of the earth and its resources, both through Adam and through Noah, but sadly, that stewardship has been flawed. Selfishness has led to carelessness and neglect, and to the exploitation of the earth and its resources. Long term sustainable usage has been sacrificed for the sake of short term profits.

So today we have extensive deforestation, contaminated land, depleted fish stocks, holes in the ozone layer, atmospheric pollution and the threat of climate change. We have the problems of famine and disease, waste and destruction due to inefficiency, and more due to wars and strife. We have congested roads and overcrowded cities, rapidly depleting fuel supplies and other valuable raw materials, and the corresponding difficulties of dealing with waste dumps, pollution, and many more problems which statesmen and scientists have to try to solve. Too often, however, developments in science and technology have been employed for harm and warfare rather than benefit and peace, for enriching the rich rather than for the betterment of the poor.

We are part of a groaning creation which still waits. People still suffer. Injustice still stalks the globe. But God is in control. His purposes will be fulfilled for the blessing of all who are willing to trust in Him. Meantime, in "holy conversation and godliness" may we be "looking for and hasting unto the coming of the day of God" (2 Pet 3.11-12), that day when every groan will have ceased, when there shall be no more curse on the fair creation of God.

CHAPTER 5

"Upheld by the Word of His Power"

All around us, wherever we look, we can see regular patterns, and systems which are under control. Man in his sin and selfwill often gets out of control, but not the natural world, for it submits to the laws of the Lord. Night follows day, summer follows spring, the moon waxes and wanes, the nearer planets and the farther constellations in the night sky follow patterns which are recognisable year after year. The times of sunrise and sunset are so regular that they can be calculated years in advance, as can the ebb and flow of the tides, accurate to within seconds. These can be traced back to the constancy of the annual orbit of the earth round the sun, its daily spin on its axis, and for the tides, the monthly lunar cycle - all of them set by their Creator.

It is the same in the living world. Look at the birds. The swallows and other summer migrants arrive on time from thousands of miles away, make their nests in the same place as last year, stay for a few months to rear their young then leave us again in late autumn. In the gardens and fields, green growth breaks through the bare earth and beautiful blossoms appear at the time you have come to expect them, before bearing fruit and withering away. In the large rivers, salmon from the ocean swim upstream and leap raging waterfalls to spawn in the very gravel beds in which they started life years before. In our own bodies, the cycles of blood circulation, breathing, food digestion are regular and so commonplace that we hardly stop to think about them (until something goes wrong!), whilst special functions like having babies are so programmed that delivery dates can be prepared for well ahead. It is all very marvellous.

Natural Laws

Those who have studied any of these matters will tell you that they follow well known laws which have been discovered over many years of observation and measurement. It is clear that everything is not in a state of chaos. Certain principles are obeyed which scientists have called natural laws. To the believer, the existence of these laws is no surprise. They originate in the wisdom of almighty God who stamps order as well as beauty on everything He does, who does everything after the counsel of His own will. All of God's creation is upheld by the word of His power (Heb 1.3). His word is not simply the law they obey; He personally has them all in control. The universe is not ruled by science, it is ruled by God.

Science provides descriptions and explanations for natural processes. Sometimes the explanations and their laws are given in terms of complex and elegant mathematics. It has even been claimed that the universe is pure mathematics. Sir James Jeans (1877-1946), a renowned English scientist/mathematician, wrote the following: [1]

"The universe appears to have been designed by a pure mathematician... If the universe is a universe of thought, then its creation must have been an act of thought. Modern scientific theory compels us to think of the creator as working outside of time and space, which are part of his creation, just as an artist (does) outside his canvas."

Jeans is among the many great thinkers who have been led to acknowledge the Creator from observing beautiful design and precise order in the universe. His language might not be what we would use to describe God, but his words exemplify the truth of Romans 1.19-20, which the inspired writer says leaves man without excuse.

God is the creator and sustainer of everything. He is superior to every law, the law-maker Himself. And all these laws, like the moral and spiritual ones, are for the benefit of all. A world which obeyed no laws would be a dangerous place, even as a lawless society would be.

The Fundamental Laws
Four fundamental laws govern the natural world [2]. It is noteworthy that their discoverers acknowledged that what they were studying were the wonderful works of God.

1. *The law of gravitation.* The best known application of this universal law is the *law of gravity* which controls all movements on earth. Sir Isaac Newton (1642-1867) who discovered it saw "the counsel and dominion of an intelligent Being, ... who is Lord of all". The related *laws of planetary motion* explain and describe how and why the earth and the other planets move round the sun in elliptical orbits. When Johannes Kepler (1571-1630) discovered these he prayed, "O God, I thank Thee that Thou hast permitted me to think Thy thoughts after Thee!"

2. *The laws of electrostatics.* Opposite charges attract each other and like charges repel, with a force which rapidly diminishes the farther apart they are. These laws, along with the related laws of electromagnetism, govern every electrical device you can think of, natural or man-made. Michael Faraday (1791-1867), one of the great pioneers in this field, was a preacher of the gospel, and honoured God in his work.

3. *The laws of thermodynamics.* These laws were deduced in the nineteenth century from studies on heat (*thermo-*) and motion or work (*dynamics*). They govern all processes, changes and reactions, whether chemical or physical, natural or technological. The first of these laws is *conservation of energy* – energy cannot be created or destroyed. So the immense power or energy in the universe must have been provided from outside of itself – as the Bible says it was. The second law governs the *production of useful work*, and shows

that when work is produced, some energy has to be wasted (e.g., in cooling an engine). These laws were formalised by Lord Kelvin (William Thomson, 1824-1907). He said, "Science positively affirms creative power."

4. *The laws of life*. The most basic of these is the *law of biogenesis* formulated by Louis Pasteur (1822-1895). It states that life can come only from previous life. Life never comes from dead matter– yet one of the key claims of evolution is that it did! This law says this would not happen! Only God can initiate life. Pasteur's work led to antiseptic surgery, pasteurisation, immunisation, and vaccination which have saved countless lives. He said, "The more I study nature, the more I stand amazed at the work of the Creator."

Law and Order

In every field of science and technology, in every application from microbiology to astronomy, from oceanography to volcanology, from computer science to crop science, and dozens more, it is law and order that prevail. If this were not so, the subjects would be impossible to study, and their benefits unavailable.

This law and order is a gift of God to His creation, as is man's intellect to discover and apply these laws. Sad to say, many of these discoveries and applications have been abused and not employed for man's benefit. Think of explosives - for digging tunnels, extracting minerals, or making bombs and landmines. Think of the uses and abuses of printing, the internet, and so on. The extra knowledge and ability now available have highlighted the basic human dilemma - how to decide between good and evil, what to use resources for, how to make the correct choice. Science can offer no guidance for this.

But for all who are willing to seek it, guidance is available. It is found in the moral and spiritual law of God: "The law of the Lord is perfect, converting the soul" (Ps 19.7). "Order my steps in Thy Word; and let not any iniquity have dominion over me" (119.133).

Those four fundamental laws of nature described above encompass many other helpful laws or principles which are used in specialised fields of science and technology, to 'spell out' the details and applications. A similar thing is seen in God's spiritual law. The Lord Jesus said that the message of the law and the prophets was contained in two fundamental commandments: to love the Lord with all the heart and the soul and the mind; and to love one's neighbour as one's self (Matt 22.36-40). "Love is the fulfilling of the law" is how Romans 13.10 puts it. Many precepts of Holy Scripture 'spell out' the details and give particular examples to apply in daily life, but the fundamental law is the law of love. It is the first and greatest commandment.

This "perfect law of the Lord" (Ps 19.7), revealed in His Word, shows us how to glorify Him and be of benefit to others. Those natural laws which we have considered, "the word of His power" (Heb 1.3), also do this. They exist for the benefit of all, although perhaps unnoticed by many. They also unerringly point to God their author, and they tell out the glory of His wisdom.

---

1. Sir James Jeans, *The Mysterious Universe*. New York, Macmillan Co., 1930
2. The laws of Relativity and of Quantum Mechanics are too specialised to describe here.

CHAPTER 6

Order and Chaos

In Genesis 1 we read how God in His wisdom and power brought order and beauty out of formless chaos. Emptiness and darkness were stage by stage replaced by what God would repeatedly call "good" and then "very good". Things would be separated from each other, an ordered, structured, beautiful world would be created, ready for man to live in.

By Genesis 3, however, it is all changing - sin and chaos are spreading as they continue to do to this day. Yet an almighty hand of grace and government controls everything. God's purpose is to head up all things in Christ, and glorify His name for ever. But Satan's purpose is to promote chaos, disorder, and disobedience to God. The increasing disorder and deterioration both in society and in the realm of creation show that everything at present is not what God designed it to be.

We have been noting recently just how different this earth has become. Creation's story is moving through the darker chapters of "bondage and corruption". They include what men call natural disasters or even "acts of God", and they say, "Why does God allow this?" God is blamed when things go wrong as they see it, but never acknowledged for His providence and provision every day, seldom thanked for His grace and goodness. There is no denying that the present chapters are very dark and acutely difficult for many, but the last ones will be as bright and beautiful as the first, even more beautiful, when

"Every trace of sin's sad story,
All the curse has passed away".
(H Bonar)

The effects of redemption will spread beyond the church and the nation of Israel to include the whole of creation. Order and beauty will yet prevail.

Entropy

The change and decay all around us can be examined using an important scientific principle called entropy. All natural processes are governed by changes in energy and entropy, and we shall look at a few examples next. We might be more familiar with concept of energy. But entropy is important, basically it means chaos or disorder. It comes from the second law of thermodynamics which we noted earlier. We shall see that in fact it negates the main proposals of evolution.

In natural processes, energy is usually given out, as when a fire burns to give out heat, or when water flowing downhill through a turbine produces electricity. The ashes and the combustion products, or the water at low level, contain much less energy than what was there at the beginning. Now in such processes, there is also more disorder at the end than at the beginning, e.g., the combustion products possess more entropy (more disorder) than the fuel and oxygen. In a different example, after salt has dissolved in water there is more entropy than before. The particles are more "mixed up" in the solution, and that is why the salt dissolves.

Even in daily life, certain things "just happen" because of an increase in entropy. Your room, your desk, your files become untidy, disorganised so easily - without any effort on your part! Or, more dramatically, a glass of water (or worse still, milk) falls off the table and the liquid plus fragments of glass "just happen" to go everywhere! (Remember 2 Sam 14.14.)There is a

41

state of chaos, disorder and even brokenness which "just happened".

The general principle is that if entropy increases, processes will occur naturally, they will "just happen" if the appropriate conditions are present. But they won't "just happen" to go in the reverse direction. Cleaning up a mess and organising things doesn't "just happen" no matter how long you leave it! Also water does not flow uphill, combustion products do not turn into fuel again, salt does not separate from water by itself. These reverse processes can be *made* to happen, e.g., water can be pumped to a higher level, tidying up can be done, but these all require a designed application of energy.

From the entropy principle, we can conclude (from experience and all known science confirms it), that the things which just happen of their own accord, are those which eventually and inevitably lead to more disorder, greater entropy. It is the increase in entropy which drives such processes forward.

Two Implications

There are at least two implications of this. The first is that the longer all the natural processes in the world or the universe go on, the more its disorder (entropy) increases. Just as time cannot be turned back, the entropy of the universe does not decrease. Because of this, entropy has been called 'time's arrow'. We observe a groaning creation obeying the second law of thermodynamics, moving in the direction of increased entropy along with decreased available energy. The total entropy, the chaos, is now greater than ever it was.

The other implication of the inevitable entropy increase in all natural processes threatens the fundamental principle of evolution which says that more complex systems or creatures "just happened" to develop from simpler ones over a long period of time. But it is contrary to the second law of thermodynamics (and to all of our experience) that simpler, disordered systems will by themselves become more complex, more organised. Order and organisation do not "just happen" to come from chaos, no matter how long it is left. As we have seen, some external intelligence and a designed application of energy or power are required to make this happen.

Take a specific example. In all living cells, many very complex substances exist (proteins, lipids, nucleic acids etc) in a water-based fluid. Life is sustained by these very complicated molecules interacting with others equally as complicated, in matching, coordinated processes. Now according to evolution, these organised molecules "just happened" to be formed from smaller and simpler ones. Also by coincidence, the other matching molecules "just happened" to be synthesised from smaller ones at that time - then DNA would be formed and life could begin! Indeed, going further back, these smaller molecules themselves "just happened" to be formed from their component atoms, and those atoms from their component particles, and so on back to nothing!! Such processes are opposed by the entropy restrictions of thermodynamics, and common sense would agree (which actually says the same things in a different language!). Synthesis and coincident, cumulative cooperation does not "just happen" unless "someone" organises it!

It is of course true that biomolecules are constantly being made in living cells, as evolutionists will point out. But notice that this biosynthesis happens only within *already living* cells. Before life is present, life cannot be sustained. An intelligent system (e.g., an enzyme) is *already* in place, "Someone" has organised it, to utilise energy and drive the reaction in the difficult direction of lower entropy (as with the water pump referred to above).

Without this, what happens of its own accord is the degradation of complex molecules into simpler ones, as we actually observe in nature over long periods of time. Old, dead vegetable or animal tissues left to themselves rot away, a natural processes which "just happens", moving in the direction of higher entropy, the *opposite* direction to what evolution requires!

Reversing the Changes

Sometimes you come across an old, ruined building. The ravages of time have made a pile of rubble from what was once a handsome structure, designed and made by someone long ago. Left to itself, any manmade structure moves in this direction of greater entropy. That is also what natural structures do, as we have been describing.

But that process can be reversed. If someone with a design plan (intelligence) and with resources (energy) works upon that pile of rubble, a beautiful structure can reappear. But it won't happen on its own! The longer it is left, the worse it gets, the more it deteriorates. We are told that evolution required thousands of millions of years to bring about the world's huge variety of life-forms, and before that, more thousands of millions of years to provide an environment for life to begin. But according to the second law of thermodynamics, *these huge lengths of time would promote* **more deterioration**, *more entropy, not more organisation and improvement*. Remember entropy is time's arrow. The longer it goes on, the more disorganised it becomes.

In the beginning God by His wisdom and power brought order and beauty out of chaos. When our Lord Jesus Christ renews this world and rules in perfection He will do this again. He will lift the curse from the earth. He will remove all the effects of sin. He will reduce the entropy. The run-down will be halted, the corruption ended, the groaning hushed to peace.

Just now sin reigns and entropy reigns too, in a world where man's ideas lead to more and more chaos. Yet in our lives and in our assemblies, for example, godly order may be found (1 Cor 14.33,40) in the measure in which the wisdom and power of the Word of God is presently and deliberately obeyed.

PART 2

THE GENESIS ACCOUNT

In which we take note of –

what happened in the beginning (Gen 1);

the huge changes which came about with the great flood (Gen 6-8);

and look at some geological facts

and the importance of fossils.

CHAPTER 7

The Days of Creation

It is now time to return to Genesis 1 to consider some of the details of this remarkable chapter. It's worth reading it again just now, if you haven't done so recently. Here is what God has revealed about the beginning, what we believe actually happened.

Hebrews 11.3 says that "by faith we understand that the worlds were framed by the word of God". It does not say, "we understand *how* ...", for we do not understand *how*. God has not revealed this to us, and even if He had, we might not have been able to comprehend it. But we do understand *that* He did it, for He has told us so. By faith we understand, because faith is our response to the revelation of God. That is solid rock foundation. There is much speculation about *how* it happened, but that is largely the shifting sand of human reasoning and research based upon present day evidence which might be totally irrelevant to the conditions of the beginning. Such speculation has no place in Genesis 1.

Some Days
There have been many debates about what a "day" was in Genesis 1 – particularly what did the word mean, or how long was each "day". Some have suggested that the days were days of revelation to Moses as he wrote about it. Others have used 2 Peter 3.8 to 'prove' that each day lasted for a thousand years. (That verse has no such meaning or application. It is simply telling us that measurement of time is totally irrelevant for God.)

Alternatively, since we read about the "day of grace", the "day of the Lord", etc., the days could be (long) periods of undefined duration. Certainly the word *day* does sometimes have that meaning. But as we shall see, these ideas did not at all help to solve the problems which were thought to exist.

More legitimately, interesting spiritual lessons have been taken from the day by day creation activities, for example to parallel the work of God in the new creation (as in Eph 2.10). Light dawns, life begins, fruit is produced, and so on. Also these days have been viewed as a picture or type of the dispensations of God's dealings with men throughout all of this world's history, moving on ultimately to the day of eternal rest.

So what was a creation day in Genesis 1? It was simply a day, the most common measurement of time recognisable by all people everywhere throughout history. The duration of hours, or even years, was not always recognisable by everyone, before clocks and calendars arrived, but the regularity of "evening and morning" could hardly be missed. God chose this well known fundamental unit of time in which to perform His different acts of creation.

This simplest and most obvious definition of a creation "day" (and simplest explanations are always best!) is confirmed by a comment made in Exodus 20.8, about Israel's Sabbath, a day of the normal week to follow six similar days: "for in six days the LORD made heaven and earth, the sea, and all that in them is, and rested on the seventh day." Consistency requires the word "day" to mean the same throughout the section. We would also have to look at the use of the word in all the early chapters of Genesis, and be consistent. For example, within ch.1 we read about the night and the day (v.5), seasons, days, and years (v.14). Also, what are "the days of [Adam's] life" (3.17), or the "forty days", "one hundred and fifty days", etc. of the flood (7.17,24)? It would be difficult, even absurd, to make them mean something other than what is obvious.

Some Difficulties

The main reason why it was thought necessary to interpret a "day" to mean something else, was to make long periods of time available for geological history which, in the nineteenth century, was (and still is) being insisted upon as factual and indisputable. No problem existed with a "day" before that. But attempts to 'extend' the day still did not fit in with the requirements of the accepted geological record, again causing more problems than they tried to solve, something akin to the Gap Theory which we dismissed earlier. We shall see in a later part of this series that geological history is best accounted for by effects of the great flood of Genesis 7. It is never a good idea to interpret the words of Scripture to fit in with man's ideas which are foreign to Scripture, and which are liable to change anyway.

Another difficulty for some people was that it just seemed to be too short a time for all that to happen! Even yet, you can detect the ridicule when they say, "You don't believe that the world was made in six days surely!" Actually we do, without apology! Notice two things about this.

First, God could have done it all in an instant if He had so wished. We need time to do things, evolutionists postulate millions of years. But He did not, He is the Almighty. In some ways it is a marvel that He took so long to do it! What He shows us is a progressive unfolding of His power and wisdom in an orderly way, a day at a time, to teach us about Himself. His method of teaching is always "line upon line, precept upon precept" (Isa 28.10). This is also how He wants us to live our lives depending on Him, a day at a time.

Second, there is a very popular theory called the Big Bang, in which it is proposed that all the matter in the universe was made in a tiny fraction of a second from one small speck of something in a huge explosion. It is strange that not a question is asked, not an eyebrow raised, at the idea of all the material of this immense universe appearing in just a tiny fraction of a second, suddenly from nowhere! A totally different mindset is applied to creation in six days by the word of God.

The Big Bang theory is popular for obvious reasons, but it is based upon very tenuous reasoning and huge extrapolations. It starts from some astronomical observations which suggest a presently expanding universe, projected back in time to when it began expanding, when it was proposed to be just a really tiny speck. It is calculated that this was billions of years ago, with no changes occurring during all that time. Where the original speck came from is not explained, nor how an explosion could suddenly just happen with no energy to drive it, nor how this explosion made something useful when every other explosion we know of destroys things! The logic of the theory is missing. Many will admit, "We do not understand it, but we believe it happened." Those who trust in the infallible Word of God can be infinitely more confident, even in the logic of it, when we say, "By faith we understand ..." Actually, if you think about it, the term "Big Bang" would much more correctly apply to the end of everything, not the beginning, according to 2 Peter 3.10.

Something Definite

As you read through Genesis 1 (again), the general picture is clear to you, as it was to the devout reader of the Scriptures in early Jewish times, to those who lived in New Testament days, in the Dark Ages and the Middle Ages, in fact through all previous centuries, BC and AD, and to most people throughout the world today. The way the chapter was written enabled it to be understood by everyone, long before a scientific language had been invented, and before a scientific age brought up its objections and posed its questions and criticisms. The chapter was written not to teach science or logic, but to teach about God and His greatness. Yet it is totally consistent with real scientific fact and logic.

Creation was a progressive set of sovereign acts by God to prepare a world fit for man to live in, to prepare a stage upon which, to reuse a well known metaphor, the great drama of redemption would be enacted. Each day brought the objective nearer. From empty chaos God produces an environment which is ideal for the man He had in mind, to live a full and fulfilling life in fellowship with Himself. By the seventh day it was finished, and God rested in fellowship with the man He had created. It was "very good".

The activities of the Creator on each day are different, as "He spake, and it was done; He commanded, and it stood fast" (Ps 33.9). But certain phrases are repeated again and again such as - "and God said", "and it was so", "and it was good". These show us the continuous connection between God's purpose, His power, and His pleasure, themes which will unfold throughout the pages of Scripture and, by matchless grace, include us.

CHAPTER 8

What God Created and Made

The inspired record of Genesis 1 contains all that we need to know about the creation of the universe. It does not contain all that we might like to know about this fascinating and interesting subject, for we are naturally curious about matters which affect us and our environment. But however much we may enquire or attempt to research and reason it out, we come up against huge difficulties. By any timescale it happened so long ago. Present conditions are very likely to be quite different from and therefore irrelevant to the conditions at the beginning because change and interruption is the norm of both human and geological history. Many theories have been proposed, but all contain huge assumptions, extrapolations and uncertainties, and as we have seen, some of the most popular ones contain errors and inconsistencies even with established knowledge.

It would be better to ask someone who knows, someone reliable who was there to observe it. During the work of creation, we read repeatedly "and God saw …". Here is the one reliable eyewitness account of it all, the only one, recorded for our benefit in as much detail as God saw we needed, and in such a way as readers of Scripture down the centuries could take in. Every attempt at filling out the details, or at proposing alternatives suffer from the great disadvantage of not being there to observe it. Science itself depends upon the recording of actual observations, what has reliably been seen and measured. In legal disputes, reliable eyewitness accounts carry much more weight than deductions, conjectures and attempted reconstructions. Because "God saw" and "it is written", we can have every confidence in the truth of Genesis 1.

Created or Made?

In Genesis 1 and 2 the word *'created'* (Heb *bara*) occurs at three specific points, in 1.1, 1.21, 1.27 (3 times), whereas the word *'make/made'* (Heb *asah*) occurs more often, five times each in chs.1&2. The words are distinguishable and their meanings diverge, but we must not read too much into this. It has been proposed that the three uses of the word *'created'* denote key stages in the work, i.e. the "heavens and the earth" on Day 1, animal life of all types on Day 5, and man on Day 6. These are clearly important, new beginnings of particular things which will feature significantly in the rest of Scripture. But we must not deduce that everything else was not new, or somehow were not created!

Words have meaning only within their contexts. So we find that *'created'* and *'made'* are often used interchangeably, even in these verses. Thus in 1.26 we read, "let us *make* man …" and in v.27 we have, "So God *created* man"; in 1.1 "God *created* the heavens and the earth" and in 2.4 "God *made* the earth and the heavens"; also in 2.3, "God *created* and *made*" (literally "created to make"). It is the same throughout the Bible, e.g., "all things were *made* by Him" (Jn 1.3), and "Thou hast *created* all things" (Rev 4.11); God is "our *Maker*" (Ps 95.6), "our *Creator*" (Eccl 12.1); "it is He that *made* us" (Ps 100.3), He "*created*", "*formed*", and "*made*" us (Isa 43.7). Thus it is not a question of anything being created *or* made, it is that everything was created *and* made. "All things were *created* by Him, and for Him" (Col 1.16) and "without Him was not anything *made* that was made" (Jn 1.3). Whichever word you use, the work is all His, and He has all the glory.

Progression and Purpose

All of God's works have a progression and a purpose, as may be traced in Genesis 1. Modern descriptions of the universe tend to emphasise its vastness, and the relative smallness of our galaxy, our solar system, our planet, and ourselves (and David thought that too, one night, see Ps 8.3-4), but the view of Genesis 1 is clearly earth-centred and indeed focussed on man from the beginning. Since we were chosen in Christ before the foundation of the world, God's plans centred on putting man into the world, it was no afterthought. But it was only when an environment suitable for him was in place that God said, "Let us make man…". So from Day 1 to Day 6 this environment was being prepared a stage at a time. Let us look at the progression of events, as these verses take us from the universe (v.1) to the dry land of earth (v.10) and to Adam and Eve (v.27).

Broadly speaking, during the first three days God was forming and fitting a home suitable for man, and in the next three He was furnishing it with fullness and variety. Man needs somewhere stable and benign, with light to see, air to breathe, water to drink, food to eat – so God provides these during Days 1, 2 and 3. The water-covered planet in total darkness is clearly unsuitable - waters must be put in their place, an expansive atmosphere and dry land are made, and a food supply got ready. But mankind will also require a means of tracking time, of having manageable amounts of it, and also a sense of direction for his travels, provided in the sky on Day 4. Man's home will be a beautiful place with a wonderful variety of other creatures all around, living and moving and breeding, myriads of them, in the sea, in the air, and on the land, made on Days 5 and 6. Man will share earth with them all, but will be different from them all, indeed given dominion over them and stewardship of them.

In addition to this, Adam himself also has a special need. He needs a helper, not to be found among even the most sociable of other creatures, but specially made by God, Eve, his true match and mate. Above all, Adam and all mankind need God, for man was made in God's likeness, with a living soul which no other creature has, able to communicate and share meaningful experiences.

So each day's work underpinned the next. Thus, light is fundamental, a form of energy upon which every natural process depends; water is necessary but it has to be in the right place; dry land with its vegetation is available as a habitat and a food source before animals and man will require them. God did it all in the correct, logical order, according to His plan and purpose.

Separation and Distinction

What an amazing change has occurred during the course of Genesis 1. By the "breath of His mouth" (Ps 33.6), the "work of His fingers" (8.3), the skill of His hand (119.73), in the wisdom of His mind (104.24), and the love of His heart God has produced a masterpiece called man in a world he can enjoy. It is all beautiful because of the separations and distinctions which God produced, different from the first monotonous black watery waste. He has separated light from darkness, water from water, day from night, kinds of living creatures from other kinds, male from female. Each of these is different because God made them that way.

"After their kind" is repeated 10 times in the chapter (and after this occurs only in Gen 6&7, Lev 11 and Deut 14, which is significant). It means that each animal, bird, fish, insect, tree, plant etc. is a distinct species. Within that species time would bring about altered characteristics in response to environmental pressures or selective breeding, but a species will not change into another one. Change within species has been observed – that is the only true evolution there is, better called adaptation. Change from one species to another, however, no matter how long a time is given, does not happen, has not been observed. That 'evolution' is speculation and theorising.

Male and female of relevant species were also created, distinct and necessary for each other and to produce future generations. Reproduction and survival of the species depends totally upon the matching and complementary functions of each from the start. Successful breeding with partly developed male and female is impossible – the species would become extinct! Evolution does not have a way round this. It is just so sensible and obvious that male and female had to be created to begin with!

The most distinct of all was man. God made other creatures in huge numbers at once, but He lovingly formed man and then woman, one unique pair. Distinguished by having a "living soul", in the likeness of God, they were special. God blessed all the creatures of the sea and the air on Day 5, but when He blessed man on Day 6 it was for a greater purpose. All God's works would praise Him (Ps 145.10), but only man could and would worship Him for ever. That is why He made us.

CHAPTER 9

The Flood and its Effects

The worldwide flood described in Genesis 6-8 must be fully taken into account in any attempt to understand and interpret the past history of the earth and its present state. When we think about the flood, for good reasons we tend to focus on the spiritual side of it, its cause and effects, and the beautiful picture of salvation from judgement in the ark which God provided. But in Scripture there are some hints as to physical effects it had upon the face of the earth, to which geology bears witness very clearly. The world was a very different place after the flood from what it was before it. Indeed that is what 2 Peter 3.6-7 tells us, as we have noted before.

The flood was an immense cataclysm of dimensions which we can hardly imagine, a dramatic change to conditions which prevailed in the earth up till then. Creative processes ended with the words of Genesis 2.1-3, God's creation was very good. But sin entered, deterioration began, and brought with it those processes which continue until now, which steadily and inevitably lead to decay and death. These are the processes to which apply the natural laws which we have already considered. Then for well known reasons which He explained before it came, God in His sovereign power superimposed on top of these this great flood using materials and forces already present and latent in the earth and its surroundings since the days of creation. It had never happened before, and it will not happen again, witness God's promise of this every time you see the pure beauty of a rainbow! (Gen 9.12-16).

Changes

The changes made by the flood were numerous and far reaching. The world would not be the same again. These changes affected mankind and subsequent generations, the type of environment in which they would now live, and the physical structure of the surface of the earth which would only be explored in detail and in depth thousands of years later.

As for mankind, after the flood the human race split into three branches which are recognisable to this day throughout the world. Whilst the Bible does trace us all back to Adam for the original sin which has passed upon all, ethnically each of us has a family tree which stretches back to one of the sons of Noah. Modern genetic marker studies have confirmed this. From Shem came Abraham and the Jewish and Arab nations; from Japheth came the broad sweep of Gentile nations spread to the farther reaches of the earth by land and sea; from Ham, came those nations which found their home in the African continent. But now to them all, the gospel of the grace of God has gone without distinction and without favour - "whosoever will may come". This was seen even in the earliest spread of the gospel, when in Acts 8 a seeking son of Ham hears of the Saviour in the desert of Gaza and obtains grace, in ch. 9 a hardened and rebellious son of Shem receives mercy on the road to Damascus, and in ch. 10 a devout son of Japheth finds peace through Jesus Christ, who is Lord of all (v.36).

Another change affecting man was the length of his life. Before the flood many hundreds of years was a normal lifetime, according to Genesis 5, but for those born after the flood this life span steadily decreased to around one or two hundred years (see Gen 11.10-26), until from the end of Genesis and into the rest of the Old Testament, few people lived beyond 100. "Threescore years and ten" or "four score" (Ps 90.10) soon became the norm, as it still is worldwide. A possible reason for all this we shall look at shortly.

Climate Contrasts

When the flood came, a truly vast amount of water fell from the skies on to the earth for forty days and nights without interruption, in addition to the upwelling of waters from beneath the earth's surface. Both of these were totally unprecedented phenomena, released by God for His "strange work" of judgement (Isa 28.21), for He delights in mercy. The waters which God had put "above the firmament" on creation day two for protection were now used for destruction as they deluged and inundated the earth.

It appears that rainfall as such was unknown before the flood, plant growth and other water needs being provided for by a cyclical "mist" which rose from the earth's surface by solar heating and returned possibly nightly (see Gen 2.5-6). Furthermore, that large amount of water which was above the aerial atmosphere ("firmament") would be in vapour form, surrounding the globe in considerable thickness. This water vapour blanket or layer would have an important effect on the earth's climate and the well being of every one of its inhabitants. Firstly it would give a "greenhouse effect" and prevent extremes of heat and cold on the earth, so that a uniformly temperate or subtropical climate could have been present all over the world, giving conditions for luxuriant growth of vegetation and survival of animals and of course man. Secondly it would filter out most of the harmful cosmic rays which bombard planet earth continuously, and also much of the harmful ultraviolet radiation, shielding everything from these particles and rays which are known to cause damage to living tissue and produce disease and ageing.

So, in antediluvian times, although the peace and beauty of Eden itself had gone, climate conditions were benign, ideal for life and growth. It is little wonder therefore that people lived so long and had large families throughout their lives. In addition animal and plant life could thrive, so that huge animals, e.g., mammoths and dinosaurs in all their variety could exist all over the world, and huge forests, grasslands, and swamps of immense variety and density would be normal, with huge specimens in them. Later, when buried and compacted during the flood, all this vegetation would provide the world's enormous coal beds, and by a different mechanism involving different organisms, vast oil fields also. We will consider fossils in some detail later, but you can readily see how all this fits together.

After the flood it was all so different across the globe. Without the shielding of the high altitude water vapour canopy, extremes of temperature and contrasting seasons would become common (see Gen 8.22, the first references in the Bible to summer and winter, cold and heat). With the drying up of the flood, mighty winds blew (8.1), surface waters would freeze, ice sheets would form and make their marks on the landscape as they moved and melted. Mankind would face a new set of difficulties which would have far reaching effects. And many plant and animal species which had been common before could exist no longer, unable to adapt to the changed environment, except for a few which found a niche in which to survive. This is when 'survival of the fittest' would really apply, and is mainly why dinosaurs and similar land giants would become extinct.

Radiocarbon Dating
How long ago all this happened is not certain, although the records of Scripture do suggest it was somewhere around 3000 BC. However, there is a method called radiocarbon dating which has given dates for certain artefacts a lot earlier than this, even back to around 10,000 BC. It works like this.

When, for example, a growing tree absorbs carbon dioxide from the atmosphere, in it there is a small amount of a radioactive form of carbon called carbon 14, which steadily decays (reduces in amount) after the wood is cut down. By measuring the small amount of carbon 14 which is in a specimen at present, and comparing this with what was there when the wood was growing, the age of the specimen can be calculated because the rate of decay is known (the 'half-life' is 5730 years). The key assumption in the calculation is that the amount of carbon 14 absorbed into the wood while it was growing long ago is the same as is being absorbed today.

Now this is highly unlikely, because the carbon 14 is produced in the upper atmosphere by cosmic rays striking nitrogen atoms. Now the intensity of these cosmic rays fluctuates over even centuries of time, but if we go back thousands of years to pre-flood conditions, additionally the thicker vapour canopy would filter out most of them. Thus much less carbon 14 would be produced to enter the growing wood, and therefore proportionately much less would be left in the specimen now. Hence if dated by this method, all samples from the era of the flood will appear to be much older than in fact they are. Thus radiocarbon dates older than about 5,000 years are in doubt, and many authorities recognise this. We recognise the reliability of the Biblical records.

of the volcanic activity on earth is found, the molten material from below erupting through weak spots.

It may have been that the continental plates were disturbed at the flood and moved apart, then their movement slowed down to its present rate. Perhaps before the flood there was only one large continent, the dry land which was created by God on Day 3 of creation week, then after the flood it was divided (Gen 10.25 speaks of the earth being divided in the days of Peleg). If you examine the main land masses on a globe, you can see that they can actually fit together like a jigsaw, and because of this, traditional geology itself proposes the existence of a single continent at one time long ago, called Pangea.

Mountains and Seas

Horizontal and lateral movements on the surface of the earth would be accompanied by vertical ones also. To accommodate the burden of water which flooded the earth, the laws of gravity would cause valleys to sink deeper and mountain ranges to rise higher as continental plates shifted and tilted. There is plenty of geological evidence that this did happen at some time in the earth's history. For example, the European Alps well over 10,000 ft in height contain rocks which were once beneath water. Marine fossils are abundant in many rocks now well above sea level. Similarly, the very deep ocean trenches could have been formed in the process by which "the waters decreased continually, ... and the tops of the mountains [were] seen" (Gen 8.5). Psalm 104.6 – 8 describes the flood and speaks of mountains going up and valleys going down, before God commands the waters not to cover the earth again. The earth's surface is now 70.8% covered by water.

There can be no doubt that the flood was a worldwide event, both from the record of Scripture, and from evidences of it which are still to be seen everywhere (more of this later). But the flood waters did not have to be 30,000 ft deep to cover Mt Everest, for example. These Himalayan ranges, along with the other main mountain chains on every continent, were probably pushed up their present elevation only as the flood receded. The flood waters just had to be deep enough to allow the ark to float above the existing and much lower mountain tops such as Ararat, with 15 cubits to spare (Gen 7.20), which, interestingly, has been calculated to be the draught of the ark [1].

Sedimentary Rocks

There are two main types of rock on the earth's surface, called igneous and sedimentary. Igneous rock was once molten, but on cooling has crystallised and solidified. Good examples are granite and basalt, chemically classed as silicates. These have most probably been little changed since their earliest creation in Genesis 1.

Sedimentary rock, on the other hand, as the name suggests is made up from small particles of sediment/sand. This rock has been formed by the effects of water creating and depositing sediments which have then been bonded together by pressure and chemical cementation. Good examples of these are limestone and sandstone. Sedimentary rock is usually found on top of igneous rock, except where volcanic activity or faults have disturbed the strata. Of special relevance to what we shall consider next, it is easy to see why fossils are found only in sedimentary rock which was once deposited by water but not in igneous rock which was once molten.

Sedimentary rock beds are of various thicknesses and are characteristically layered, as you can see in many cliffs and quarries. There is no doubt that the layers were formed and deposited by the action of water, and from the viewpoint of Scripture, this would occur on at least two separate occasions.

The first of these would be during creation week, when dry land emerged from a water-covered globe. On top of the cooled igneous bedrock would accumulate layers of eroded sediment, to settle and solidify. This sedimentary rock would contain no fossils, because there were no living things to get buried in the silt. Many large thick beds of this type of rock exist in many places with no fossils in them.

The second occasion would be the flood, when as outlined above, huge masses of sediment would accumulate and be compressed, repeatedly as the waters ebbed and flowed, in layers which would eventually show separate boundaries. Significantly this time, all kinds of living creatures and vegetation would be rapidly buried in silt and sediment. They would be fossilised by this process, so that these layers would contain fossils of different kinds of creatures depending upon where they were when the flood waters overtook them. There they would remain until uncovered by excavations in recent times. Geologists would classify these fossil-bearing rocks according to the time scale required by the theory of evolution, but to us they present an awful record in stone of divine judgement upon the sin of an ancient world.

We will examine the fossil record next, to see what it tells us about a world that perished in the great flood. We will also see how the evidence of the fossils does not point to evolution after all, but is far better explained by the ideas described in the above paragraphs.

---

1. For more details see *And God Said* by F Abou Rahme (Ritchie Publications), and *The Genesis Flood* by JC Whitcomb and HM Morris (Baker Book House) – undoubtedly the authoritative and key reference work on this subject.

CHAPTER 11

Fossils and the Flood

Fossils are the remains of plants and animals cast in stone, often showing in remarkable detail what they looked like. Some are very similar to present day species and can be recognised as such, whilst many others belong to species now extinct. They are a silent witness to something which happened long ago, something unusual, something catastrophic. They are evidence of life, and of sudden death.

Usually when a plant or animal dies, it decays very rapidly and leaves very little evidence of what it looked like. Normal burial, or predators in the wild, ensures that within a short time perhaps only a few hard bones remain. Fossils, however, can show the soft tissue of animals, feathers of birds, scales of fishes, bark on tree trunks, intricate patterns of tracery on leaves, ferns, flowers and such like. And furthermore, fossils are plentiful, existing on every continent, sometimes covering many square miles in area and many feet deep in the rock strata. So how are fossils formed?

It is almost universally agreed that fossils are formed in flood conditions, by rapid burial of the creatures and vegetation in flood-borne silt. Rapid burial ensures preservation intact, while mineral-rich water soaks into the structure and ensures permanence. Increasing pressure from above casts everything into stone – literally petrifying it for good. So there these ancient creatures lie until the quarryman or the miner or the geologist uncovers them for the modern world to wonder about and theorise!

Fossils and Evolution Theory

It is widely taught and therefore commonly believed that the fossil record provides the evidence for evolution. The proposal is that over millions of years different types of creatures which then existed were fossilised during different prehistoric floods, and so the rocks contain a record of different forms of life and show how they changed over that period of time. Visit almost any museum and you will find this popular story spelt out, along with many graphic but totally imaginary representations of prehistoric conditions, describing shallow seas where now there is land, followed by continental movements, the slipping of strata, and so on.

Evolution theory is taken as true, as the basis and the starting point. The facts (i.e. the fossil specimens) are arranged to fit the theory, and to draw further conclusions. A typical example is the following, taken recently from a museum in Yorkshire: *Because plants and animals evolve over time, we can use fossils to estimate the age of the rocks.* But wait a minute! If they did not evolve, fossils cannot tell anything about the age of rocks! An unproved theory is being used to produce data which are presented as facts!

Take for example the Devonian Old Red Sandstone in northern Scotland. It is said to be 700 million years old *just because* it contains many fossilised fish which *evolution says* existed *then*. But next we are also told that the age of a fossil is given by the type of rock in which it is found. So if another fossil is found in Old Red Sandstone, we are told that the *fossil* is 700 million years old because it was found *there*. This is circular reasoning, and is not really science! Rocks and fossils *cannot* be correctly dated from each other!

Nevertheless, *based on the assumption that evolution is true*, a "geological column" has been built up showing strata of many different types with "key" fossils in them, going back something like 1,000 million years. It is then taught dogmatically that this is the record of the progressive evolution of the different life forms on earth, from lowly water-dwelling creatures at the bottom, through fishes, amphibians and reptiles, all the way to mammals and then man at the top.

There are, however, major difficulties and inconsistencies which are not usually mentioned! Some of the more serious ones are as follows.

- The whole geological column, bottom to top, does not exist in any one place on earth. Sections exist in different places, some large, some small. The complete column exists only in textbooks, posters and charts!
- There are many examples of "inversions", where layers of "old" rocks lie on top of "young" ones, instead of the younger ones being on the top.
- Many examples exist where fossils in the same layer of rock are of creatures which the theory says lived millions of years apart. They appear to be in the wrong place, alongside each other!
- Evolution requires many partly changed/evolved creatures to have existed at various times. But fossils of these have never been found in spite of really keen searching. Fossils are always distinct, recognisable species of animals and plants such as presently exist. The "missing links" are still missing!
- The "earliest" fossils are already very complex specialised creatures, e.g., trilobites, and they are so plentiful and so diverse that this is called the "Cambrian explosion" of life. Beneath them (pre-Cambrian) there are no fossils at all. No simpler creatures exist except in the imagination of the evolutionist.

It is actually very difficult to fit the theory of evolution around the *facts* of geology, based on what *is* found in the rocks and what *is not* found. But evolution is presented as the truth, not the first or the last time that a lie is taken to be the truth (Rom 1.25; 2 Thess 2.11-12).

Fossils and the Flood
The facts of geology fit neatly into the framework of the biblical, historical, worldwide flood of Noah's day. Just recall what we are told about the onset, duration, and upheavals of the flood which we have recently considered, then apply normal, scientific laws and principles to the situation - and it makes wonderfully good sense. In fact this was how the majority of early scientists and thinkers viewed it before evolution theory high-jacked the establishment then brain washed everyone to accept it.

Here is the basic picture to work on. As the great flood advanced, the first creatures to be killed and buried would be the least mobile, in fact those which lived in the shallow seas and around the shore line. The more mobile ones would escape higher up until their temporary refuge was inundated by water, and then they would perish. The last to succumb would be the most mobile animals and birds at the highest levels. As different types of creature were swept away into the flood, rushing water and sediment would quickly bury them in conditions which were just right for fossilisation. All this fits the observed geological facts, and it is simple and straightforward!

Thus the geological column, where it exists, is not a historical record of how creatures developed over millions of years. It is rather a record of where and when they lived and died when the flood came and destroyed them all. The order of their burial and fossilisation is according to their habitat, aquatic life first - the bottom dwellers like shells and trilobites, followed by the fishes, in huge shoals buried in contorted swimming positions which the fossils show. Then the shoreline amphibians and the slow reptiles are overcome and buried, and eventually the mammals, often in huge numbers as they herded together in the race to escape, as testified by vast fossil beds worldwide.

Superimposed onto this basic picture, we now have to think about hydrodynamic activity, the effects of vigorously moving water. Agitated, swirling water deposits objects according to their density (heaviness), so that sand, silt, gravel and everything else in the water are deposited and sorted out according to their weight and their shape. This stirring, mixing and settling would further redistribute dead creatures in the silt and allow those from different habitats to be sometimes buried together then fossilised in the same layer.

Furthermore, seismic (earthquake) activity in the earth's crust beneath the water as the flood subsided would thrust some layers up while others go down, giving the fault and slip lines common throughout the world, with the fossils they contain similarly displaced. Additionally, volcanic activity would disturb and tilt the strata, with molten rock forcing its way up through sedimentary layers to give the lava fields and basalt intrusions which we find today.

The world's vast coalfields would also be formed at this time. The luxuriant carbon rich forests, swamps and grasslands of the antediluvian era would be quickly uprooted, flattened, waterborne then buried and compacted into coal. Oil and gas too would be produced and trapped in porous rock in a similar way, from marine organisms and from decay of vegetation. (Compare methane production from landfill sites today – a small scale example of this process.)

Conclusion

Why are these basic ideas not acceptable to so many people? Why is an unfounded and conjectural theory favoured so much?

The fossils preach worldwide that the wages of sin is death. Instead of recognising them as a permanent record of divine judgement upon a wicked world, and heeding their warning, people explain them away. Those who serve sin and Satan do not want to be reminded that God will have the last word. The Flood is the prototype of the greater judgement to come (2 Pet 3.5-6; Matt 24.37-39).

PART 3

SOME UNIQUE AND AMAZING FACTS

In which we describe

the wonderful handiwork of God seen in –

the precise suitability of earth for life and for man;

the unique synchronized properties of water and light

and the chemistry of life;

this environment carefully planned and created for man;

the extraordinary uniqueness of man;

the amazing complexity and efficiency of features

in our own bodies.

CHAPTER 12

The Earth – a Unique Planet

The world we live in, this planet called Earth, is truly a unique place, an exceptional planet among all the others in the solar system, an exceptional world among all the uncountable worlds in space. It is exceptional and unique in at least two respects. The first and best of these is that the very Son of God came here, born in a lowly manger at Bethlehem, dying on a rugged cross at Calvary, to work out God's great plan of salvation. He "came *into the world* to save sinners" (1 Tim 1.15), to provide eternal life. The second unique feature is how Earth alone provides an environment which is just right to contain and support physical life.

Although many changes took place at and after the great flood which we have been considering, these affected mainly its surface structure, its topography, geography and geology, rather than its fundamental properties designed by God. We have already seen that His creative acts in Genesis 1 were in an orderly sequence leading up to the point where man could take his place in an 'up and running' world which he could enjoy and care for, which would supply all his requirements for food, home, peace and beauty. In spite of the entrance of sin into the world, the fact remains that those strict and stringent conditions for life are still found on earth, and nowhere else! Scripture teaches clearly that God designed the world to be inhabited by man (Isa 45.18; Acts 17.26). We know also that the blessing of man was planned "before the foundation of the world" (Eph 1.4). Therefore God designed, founded and formed this unique planet with man in mind from the beginning.

Creation's story is written throughout the whole universe, with more being revealed and in measure understood as time passes. But most clearly for us, and most relevant to us, is the part of this amazing story written in the structure and properties of our own planet Earth. All who have studied this fascinating subject have come to the conclusion that Earth is a truly unique place, exactly suited for life and for man. Many far fetched and fuzzy theories of how it came to be like this have been proposed. A series of accidents, a few coincidences, and a measure of "luck" (and I quote from a recent science-based book!) we are told were responsible! The idea of "intelligent design" is ferociously rejected although it is so evident from the largest to the smallest structure which is explored.

Conditions for Life

Life is very fragile, although we take it for granted. Its existence depends upon many physical conditions being just right, e.g., temperatures between about 0 and 40 °C, and values of fundamental gravitational and nuclear forces being what they are. It also depends on certain chemicals being available, e.g., water and oxygen, and equally on others being absent or in very small amounts, e.g., cyanide and carbon monoxide. Likewise there are forms of radiation which are absolutely essential to all life on earth, i.e., "visible" light and some infrared, but others are lethal, e.g. X rays and deep ultraviolet.

In the next few chapters, we shall look at the unique way in which *all* these conditions come together in our planet, and nowhere else, how God designed them into the fabric of the world we live in, how conditions in the universe are *"just right"* for life. This has been expounded in detail by a modern physicist, Paul Davies, who called it "The Goldilocks Enigma".

The Sun

The earth's surface temperature is governed mainly by two things, the energy emission from the sun and the distance from the sun. If the sun were hotter, or if Earth were nearer it, all life would burn up. If it were cooler, or Earth farther away, all would freeze to death.

The sun is a star whose energy is generated from its interior where hydrogen atoms combine to form helium atoms at a temperature of around 15 million °C. Its surface temperature is about 5,500 °C. Stars vary in size from about one tenth to over one hundred times the size of the sun, and their surface temperatures vary between 3,000 and 40,000 °C (shown by their colours – red dwarfs up to blue-white giants). Among all these, the sun is a medium sized yellow star (diameter about 865,000 miles, 109 times the diameter of the earth, 745 times the mass of all the planets put together). At the correct distance of just about 93 million miles from the sun, Earth receives the correct amount of radiation from this correct size of star to achieve the correct temperatures we can live with - all beautifully matched!

The Solar System
The sun provides the anchor point for the whole solar system of eight major planets moving round it in an anticlockwise direction, while they also spin on their own axes. There are four inner planets, Mercury to Mars, relatively small, dense and rocky; and four outer ones, Jupiter to Neptune, which are huge spheres of low density gaseous material. Planets closer to the sun are very much hotter, those farther away much cooler. Our distance from the efficient, clean, giant power generator called the sun is just right, and the energy comes free over the vast distance involved, in fact taking 8.3 minutes to reach us. "There is nothing hid from the heat thereof" (Ps 19.6). "He maketh His sun to rise on the evil and the good" (Matt 5.45).

Planets nearer the sun orbit round it faster - a year on Mercury is about a quarter of our year (whilst its "day" lasts for 58 of our days). More distant planets orbit the sun more slowly - Neptune's year is 165 of our years (its day is 16.1 hours). Among the planets, Earth occupies its unique God-given position between Venus and Mars, with even the length of the year and the length of the day suiting our life cycle.

Other factors help to maintain the temperatures we need. First the period of 24 hours for the earth to spin on its axis is just about right. Longer periods would give time for extremely cold nights and extremely hot days to develop; shorter periods would destabilise weather patterns and cause the gases of the atmosphere to spin off into space. Also, because the earth's axis is not at right angles to the sun's rays but tilted by 23.5 degrees, the energy influx is spread over a wider area north and south of the equator. Seasons are thus extended, and the very hot and the very cold regions of the earth are minimised.

As the planets orbit the sun, they trace out an elliptical path. Some, like Mercury nearest the sun or Pluto farthest away, have very elongated ellipses. But the earth's orbit is almost circular. If it too were elongated (more squashed), then for some months of the year the earth would be nearer the sun and get very much hotter, followed by very much colder months when it was further away. Such life threatening extremes do not occur because of the near circular shape of the earth's orbit.

The Atmosphere
Yet another factor which has a major effect on temperature is the size and composition of the atmosphere – an insulating blanket which helps to retain the heat ("greenhouse effect"). Atmospheres on other planets are very different. Mercury's is so thin that the temperature swings between - 170 and + 400 °C as heat is lost or gained easily. Venus's is very thick, composed of carbon dioxide, with clouds made of 80% sulphuric acid. It retains so much heat that the temperature is 475 °C.

The composition of our atmosphere is governed by the gravitational pull of the earth, as is the mobility of everything on its surface. If, for example, gravity was much less, oxygen, nitrogen and water vapour necessary for life would escape into space, only argon and carbon dioxide remaining. The shielding effect of the atmosphere would also be reduced, both for retaining heat and for preventing damage due to cosmic rays. On the other hand, if gravity was much greater, the air density and pressure would increase, and life forms of all types would require greater muscle and skeletal strength to move and survive.

Gravitational factors govern the pull of the earth on everything, especially the moon our nearest celestial neighbour. Its pull in turn affects the ocean tides, the size of which are important. Too much would give coastal instability, too little would hinder recycling of nutrients and pollutants.

The balance of *every* factor responsible for Earth being a suitable home for man, and for countless other life forms, is truly a clear pointer to the wisdom and design of the Creator. We can say with conviction and with worship, "O Lord, how manifold are Thy works! In wisdom hast Thou made them all: the earth is full of Thy riches. So is this great and wide sea ..." (Ps 104.24-25).

CHAPTER 13

"He Made the Stars Also"

Before considering more of the properties of our environment which have made it uniquely suitable for life, we should take a look beyond the confines of earth and beyond the solar system. Creation's story and God's glory is written across the skies, a silent but constant and clear declaration of His eternal power and Godhead. "The heavens declare the glory of God; ... Night unto night sheweth knowledge. There is no speech and there are no words, yet their voice is heard." (Ps 19.1–3, JND).

Some clear, dark night, go out again and look up. If you get away from the stray light from towns and cities you can see the myriads of stars much clearer, set in the velvet black darkness. Look all around you from the faint horizon to the sharper zenith, from north to south or east to west, and let the beauty and grandeur of that panorama fascinate you and move your soul. Even if you can recognise only a few of the named stars or constellations, or none of them, there is an awe-inspiring vastness and glory about it all. Like a huge billboard across the night sky it delivers a message which no one can erase, which everyone can read, proclaiming God!

If you do this, you will be doing what God commanded many others to do long ago. Remember *Abraham* (Gen 15.5 – "Look now toward heaven and tell the stars"); *Job* (9.7-10 – "God ... which alone spreadeth out the heavens, ... Arcturus, Orion, and Pleiades "); *Eliphaz* (Job 22.12 - "Behold the height of the stars, how high they are!"); *David* (Ps 8.3 – "When I consider Thy heavens, the work of Thy fingers, the moon and the stars which Thou hast ordained "); *Isaiah* (40.26 – "behold who hath created these things: that bringeth out their host by number "); also the *wise men* from the east (Matt 2.2), and *Paul* and the seamen who looked in vain for the constellations to facilitate navigation through those stormy nights (Acts 27.20).

Astronomy has developed greatly like other branches of science in the last two centuries, but it is an ancient subject, as the quotes above show. Records left by Assyrian, Babylonian, Chinese, and Arabian peoples are valued today to compare with recent observations. Measurements, predictions, and theories now dominate the subject, but the wonder of it is timeless. Consider a few of the more obvious features of the starry skies.

The Number of the Stars

God said to Abraham, "if thou be able to count them" (ref above). If you had the patience and ability, with the naked eye you could count up to about 3,000 stars in one hemisphere. That means there are around 6,000 stars visible from earth. But Galileo with his home-made telescope was able to see ten times more, up to 60,000. As telescopes improved in power and resolution, the number kept increasing. It was over 600,000 in the1850s. Now with the advent of radio astronomy it is literally uncountable! – exactly as God had said! (Jer 33.22). It is estimated that our local Milky Way Galaxy alone contains over 200 thousand million stars. And there may be over 100 million galaxies out there in space!

But why so many? To tell us of the greatness of the God who created them all by His word. He made all these millions upon millions of stars as easily as making one. He can count them, and "not one faileth" (Isa 40.26). They are all different - their variety proclaims God's glory. "Lo, these are parts of His ways" (Job 26.14); "His greatness is unsearchable" (Ps 145.3).

Varieties of Stars

Even as no two blades of grass, no two snowflakes, no two creatures are exactly the same, so no two stars are the same – they differ from each other "in glory" (1 Cor 15.41). They have different colours, brightnesses, sizes, temperatures, speeds of rotation, and compositions. We see them in different arrangements or patterns called constellations, each star a different distance from Earth.

The nearest star is called alpha Centauri (not seen in northern hemisphere, it is one of the 'pointers' to the Southern Cross). It is 4.3 light years distant, and is the third brightest star we can see. The brightest one is Sirius, readily seen from the UK as a greenish twinkling star quite low in the southern sky. It is 8.7 light years distant, and is actually 26 times as bright as the sun which is only 8.3 'light *minutes*' away, so the sun *appears* much brighter. There is another star called eta Carinae which is 4 million times as bright as the sun and over 100 times more massive, but at 6,400 light years away it is not even visible to the naked eye.

The largest star known is called Rasalgethi, about 500 light years distant. Taken with its gas cloud, its diameter is over twenty times that of the whole solar system. It is a 'red giant', with a blue-green companion orbiting around it. It is in the northern sky, in the fifth largest constellation called Hercules. The smallest star recognised is a white dwarf, half the size of the moon, at 100 light years distant.

The Constellations

For mapping purposes, astronomy now divides the sky into 88 constellations or sections. But constellations were first recognised by the ancients as groups of stars, named mostly after figures in Greek mythology. Ptolemy (150 AD) compiled a list of 48, which was later expanded as travellers observed the southern sky. We have already mentioned Orion, Hercules, and the Southern Cross. The Plough or Great Dipper is well known, directing observers to the north pole star, Polaris, which is a yellow supergiant about 650 light years away. These are all beautiful to recognise and admire.

Some constellations grouped together make up the twelve signs of the Zodiac which are used to describe where the sun appears to be during each of the twelve months of earth's yearly orbit. These have been manipulated into a superstitious system called astrology, derived from ancient paganism, totally misleading and explicitly condemned in Scripture (e.g., Isa 47.13). The proliferation of horoscopes in newspapers and magazines shows, however, that many people still follow it.

It has been said that the constellations of the Zodiac tell the story of redemption in great detail, from Virgo, the promise of the Redeemer's advent, through to Leo, His ultimate triumph [1]. Some constellations such as Libra, the Scales, and Crux, the Southern Cross, may more easily illustrate truths from Scripture [2]. But actually, a lot of imagination is often required to match the patterns of the stars in the constellations to their names, most of which are strange to us anyway. It is much simpler and better to take heed to the "more sure word of prophecy" (2 Pet 1.19), and to enjoy the full, final and clearest revelation of God in Christ Himself (Heb 1.1).

The Vastness of Space
The Milky Way to which our solar system belongs is around 100,000 light years in diameter. Sometimes on a clear night you can see it stretching right across the sky from one side to the other. With the naked eye three more galaxies can be seen, the two Clouds of Magellan and the Andromeda Galaxy apparently 2.25 million light years distant. This is the most distant object in the universe observable by the naked eye. In addition, there are nebulae, quasars, pulsars, black holes and the like which we cannot describe here.

These distances and numbers are really too huge to grasp, as is the vastness of empty space. In fact, it is now admitted that the structure and dimensions of space are beyond our comprehension. More questions than answers remain, the subject is so complex.

The observations which astronomers make involve such tiny quantities that errors can be significant. Also the conclusions reached depend upon certain laws and principles which are valid on earth but, as we have seen before, may not be valid when extrapolated over such huge distances with entirely unknown conditions. Astronomy pushes science to the limit of its methodology, and therefore confidence in the detail of its conclusions must be less than in most other sciences.

What is Man?

In the face of such vastness, such numbers of stars, the question of Psalm 8.4 arises again. Is man just an insignificant speck on a small rotating planet in one of many huge swirling galaxies? Far from it! Only man has the ability to explore, to understand and to appreciate the grandeur of the universe, and from it to learn more of the glory of its Creator and worship Him. That is our real significance and purpose!

---

1. "The Companion Bible" (E W Bullinger), Appendix 12 – a very detailed treatment.
2. See "Stars and their Purpose", ch 8; W Gitt, CLV publishers, 1996 & 2000

CHAPTER 14

Water – a Unique Liquid

We have already noticed that Earth is a unique planet having the correct surface temperature for life to exist, the heat from the sun being balanced by its distance away from us. This distance in turn depends upon the mass of the earth, which, if heavier would be nearer and hotter; if lighter would be farther away and colder. This surface temperature allows water to exist as a liquid, the only form which can support life. Freezing solid ice or scalding gaseous steam would not do.

Of all the substances we find on earth, by far the most common one is water, most of it in large quantities. Although we take it for granted, it is a remarkable substance uniquely designed and essential to sustain life. Those who (vainly) search for the existence of life elsewhere, e.g., on other planets, look for water as their first clue. Without water, there can be no life. Most of the matter in the universe consists of very hot gases (in the stars) or as deeply frozen solids (in the outer planets). Although so common on earth, water is extremely scarce in the universe. Earth is often described as "the watery planet". Just over 70% of its surface is covered by water. In vapour form it also pervades the atmosphere. Even those areas which we call dry or arid still contain significant amounts of water.

There are several special properties of water which make it truly unique and necessary for natural life. Before we look at these, remember how in Scripture water often represents what is necessary for spiritual life. Water is a figure of the Holy Spirit without whom no spiritual life is possible (John 3.5; 4.14; 7.38-

39). The "washing of water by the word" (Eph 5.26) is necessary for the maintenance of spiritual life and the fulfilment of God's purpose for us. The last invitation in the Bible is "whosoever will, let him take of the water of life freely" (v.17). Even in the spiritual deserts of this world, the soul of the believer can be like "a watered garden" (Isa 58.11; Jer 31.12). For this we must be nourished constantly by the "upper and nether springs" of the Spirit and the Word.

Properties of Water

Each of the chemical and physical properties of water makes it a key substance to support life at every level. The tiny single microscopic cell cannot function without it, nor can the large mammals on land and in the sea. All types of vegetation need it too, from the scrub of the deserts to the luxuriant growth of the tropical rain forests. It is required for the obvious necessities of drinking and irrigation, and for diffusion and distribution of nutrients and energy. It also very efficiently controls the temperature on earth and in all living things which can only survive if temperatures do not vary greatly. The special molecular structure of water gives it critical thermal properties.

Thermal Properties

Liquid water is able to absorb heat without a large increase in its own temperature, and this heat is retained efficiently. It can also release heat in large amounts without a large fall in its temperature. Water is better at doing this than any other common substance – it is said to have a high heat capacity. Life benefits from this in two ways.

First, the large oceans keep temperatures on earth steady, not rising or falling too much. Oceans are also great reservoirs and conductors of heat. Great ocean currents like the Gulf Stream transfer vast amounts of heat from the equator to the cooler latitudes, so that the climate of countries like the UK is moderated.

Second, when we are exposed to heat or cold, the temperature of our bodies is kept fairly steady because they are made up of about 70% water (as are many animals). This effect is again due to the high heat capacity of water. It is, however, further assisted by another of its properties - its heat of vaporisation is also high. This means that when liquid water is changed into vapour a lot of heat is used up. Thus when our bodies need to lose heat quickly, water is evaporated in our breath and through our skin – as heavy perspiration in extreme cases, allowing our bodies to maintain their stable temperature. A lot of heat can be removed with the loss of only a small amount of water. Water is the only substance which can do this so well.

Properties of Ice

It is commonplace to notice how water forms ice when it freezes, and to notice the ice floating on top of the water. But it is most unusual for the solid form of any substance to float on top of its liquid at the freezing point - most solids sink to the bottom because they are more dense ("heavier") than the liquid. But not ice – it is less dense than water at 0 °C where it freezes, so that unlike almost every other substance, ice floats on the surface of water.

This unusual behaviour is extremely important for all types of aquatic life. If ice did sink to the bottom when it formed, the body of water would freeze from the bottom upwards until it all became solid, and every living thing in the water would be pushed to the top where it would freeze to death. As it is, ice forming on the top acts as an insulating layer to prevent the colder air from affecting the underlying water which remains above freezing point, at around 4 °C where water has its greatest density.

It is another amazing thing that solid water (ice) is such a good insulator, because liquid water is actually a very good conductor of heat, four times better than any other common liquid. This high conductivity is another factor which further helps water to regulate and distribute heat in the oceans and in our bodies as described above. All of its properties work together for the benefit of life.

Solvent and Diffusion Properties

A vast range of different substances can dissolve in water, although to different extents. Water has been called the universal solvent. Therefore water can dissolve many substances and take them from one place to another, for example to provide nutrients and remove wastes efficiently in all types of living systems and in the larger environment. This is another of the key reasons why living systems need water.

Water can dissolve large amounts of salt and sugar. It can also dissolve a lot of carbon dioxide, and this helps to remove this gas from our bodies and controls the acidity of our fluids. It also dissolves oxygen, another substance critical for life. Our lungs absorb oxygen gas directly from the air. There it dissolves in the blood in a specially efficient way to transfer it quickly to where it is needed by cells and muscles. Life in the waters requires dissolved oxygen for breathing through gills. Dissolved oxygen is also critical for water purification – to oxidise contaminants into relatively harmless substances so that the water is freed from pollutants and can be reused. The truly versatile nature of water enables each form of life to thrive in its own habitat.

Some other properties of water enhance its unique suitability to support life. Its viscosity is low enough (not like treacle or oil) to enable it to pass easily through very small tubes such as blood capillaries. Diffusion through water is fast enough for essential materials to reach the required sites, e.g., oxygen goes through a body cell in one hundredth of a second. Its surface tension allows it to spread on certain types of surfaces but not others. You could not get a better substance than water to support life. Indeed water incorporated into the design for life is an eloquent testimony to the Creator's wisdom.

The Water Cycle

Water on earth is constantly being cycled and recycled as the heat of the sun evaporates surface water into the atmosphere from which it falls again in the form of rain, snow or dew, eventually to return to the sea. Solomon observed this long ago (see Eccl 1.7). The cycle desalinates, purifies and distributes the water for the use of all living things. It has been calculated that the atmospheric water is changed and recycled about 40 times per year, that is on average almost every week. While it is in the atmosphere it assists global warming, without which surface temperatures on earth would be below freezing, and nothing could live.

This special substance called water uniquely supports life here and now. But it will also to do so in the millenial earth as "living waters" go out from Jerusalem (Zech 14.8). And flowing from the throne of God, the "pure river of water of life" will ensure the eternal freshness of the new Jerusalem above (Rev 22.1).

CHAPTER 15

Light – a Unique Illumination

Without light, there can be no life. Natural and spiritual life both depend upon it. God's first creative act was to bring light into a scene of dark chaos: "And God saw the light, that it was good" (Gen 1.4). In the spiritual realm also He has acted, delivering us from "the power of darkness" (Col 1.13) and making us "light in the Lord" (Eph 5.8).

To be effective, light requires at least three things - a source, a receptor, and no barrier in between. The primary source of every kind of light is God Himself: "God is light, and in Him is no darkness at all" (1 Jn 1.5). If God had not sent "the true light" into the world (Jn 1.9), we would have been lost in the darkness for ever. How grateful we ought to be that "the darkness is past, and the true light now shineth" (1 Jn 2.8), and how diligently we ought to "let our light so shine before men", without barriers ("bushels") so that people around us may see our "good works and glorify our Father which is in heaven" (Mt 5.15,16).

But this light will be ineffective if no one or nothing receives it. Sad to say, Satan has blinded the minds of those who do not believe "lest the light of the glorious gospel of Christ … should shine unto them" (2 Cor 4.4). But the gracious and great Physician who opened many blind eyes while He was here on earth, and gave clarity of vision (Mk 8.25), continues to do so still by the power of the Holy Spirit and through His servants (Acts 26.18; Eph 1.18). May the example of John the Baptist inspire us, to be a "burning and a shining light (lamp)" (Jn 5.35), not the source of the light but bearers of it, voices crying, signposts pointing (Jn 1.23,29), preaching not ourselves, but Christ Jesus the Lord (2 Cor 4.5).

What is Light?
The light to which we are accustomed every day is a special and unique form of energy, coming from certain natural or artificial sources and received by our eyes. The resulting information then registered in our brain is very complex and rich in content. Variable colours, shapes and intensities all convey different meanings. Of all our senses, sight is the one which gives us most information about our surroundings.

Light is a form of radiation, which really means it is radiated or emitted from some high energy source. For life on earth, the commonest and most important source is the sun. Its heat warms us, its light sustains us and enables us to learn and discover what is around us. But that great source would have been ineffective if the light had been blocked somehow, or if we (and other life forms) were not equipped with efficient receptors of the light which arrived. In fact, the characteristics of these receptors (our eyes) match the light source exactly, and what is in between is not a barrier but an effective filter for the light. It is another example of a wonderfully designed scheme in which we can trace the wisdom and skill of our Almighty God.

What we call light is a very small section of a huge spectrum of radiation called electromagnetic waves which travel at the incredible speed of 299,793 km/sec. At one end of this spectrum the radiation has very long wavelengths. Those with wavelengths up to several kilometres are the radio waves, those with about 1 cm wavelength are called microwaves. These all carry very small amounts of energy. At the other end is the very short wavelength radiation, the X rays and the gamma rays, which carry large amounts of energy. In the middle is the visible spectrum, made up of colours to which our eyes are sensitive, the familiar 'colours of the rainbow' with all their beauty. Beyond its red end with a longer wavelength lies the infra red, and beyond its violet end with a shorter wavelength is the ultraviolet. We cannot see either of these but we can feel the effects of both, one as heat, the other as what tans our skin when exposed to the sun.

Visible Light

All types of radiation exist throughout space, but we and other life forms on earth can use only the light in the visible spectrum. Just as important, we need protection from the other radiation. Some of the longer wavelengths are harmful to life (the microwaves), and the shorter wavelengths are lethal because their energy is so great – they would and do break up our cells and tear apart the molecules which compose them. Isn't it amazing that earth receives very little of these harmful wavelengths, whilst receiving large amounts of visible radiation - which is just a tiny fraction of all the types which exist! The Creator and Sustainer of life on earth makes it happen in the following way.

First the sun which God created emits radiation with the very wavelengths which life on earth requires. With its surface temperature of about 6,000 °C it emits radiation most strongly in the middle of our visible range. We have already seen how the sun gives the earth the correct temperature for life to exist, but now we notice that its radiation is the very type that our eyes respond to. In addition, it is the type of radiation which drives reactions in our environment to provide basic food supplies, in processes which are called photobiology or photochemistry. It also emits some radiation in the near infrared which provides the significant heating effect for earth, and some in the near ultraviolet which is also utilised in some photochemical processes.

Next, as the radiation arrives at the outer boundaries of the earth, some is filtered out by ozone and by water vapour high in the upper atmosphere. What is filtered out is most of the harmful short wave ultraviolet, most of the higher energy gamma rays from outer space, and most of the longer and harmful microwaves. Thus a barrier of water vapour is in place to protect earth from most of these harmful types of radiation. But water does not absorb visible light so this useful and beneficial radiation continues on its way to reach the earth's surface.

What coincidences! - entirely different processes, one in the sun millions of miles away, the other here in the earth's atmosphere, and another example of the uniquely beneficial properties of water. "O Lord, how manifold are Thy works! In wisdom hast Thou made them all!" (Ps 104.24).

Water and Light
This interaction of light with water also benefits aquatic life. The small amount of ultraviolet which does reach the earth's surface is quickly absorbed in the very top few millimetres of the water, protecting those many organisms and creatures which live in the seas, lakes and rivers. But the visible light essential for photosynthesis is not absorbed and can penetrate down to about 100 metres.

Infrared is also absorbed in the top layers of water, heating them from the top, so that they become lighter than the lower layers. The warmer water therefore remains near the surface, preventing the mass of the water from overheating and losing much of its vital oxygen content. The surface layers also transfer heat to the air, influencing the climate, and helping to maintain steady temperatures. If the heat had gone down into the bulk of the water, this could not happen.

Sight and Light
The eye is a remarkable structure, operating in a way similar to (but much better than) a modern camera. Light enters through an automatically adjusting aperture called the pupil, is focused

by a variable lens on to the retina and registers a signal by a tiny photochemical reaction. Only the wavelengths of visible light can trigger this reaction – other wavelengths would not do so.

Furthermore, for optimum performance and clarity of vision using the wavelengths of visible light, the size of our eyes is correct. Longer wavelengths would have required much larger eyes to do the same - if wavelengths were ten times greater, the 'eye' would need to be about 25 cm in size. On the other hand, shorter wavelengths would be absorbed in the fluids of the eye, and even destroy its biological tissue and the photoreceptors on the retina. For clear vision using light from the sun, the best size is the very size of the eyes God designed and gave us, which is neither too big for the head, appearing grotesque, nor too small to be insignificant.

Sight and light and vision are wonderful gifts from God. But may nothing dim our spiritual vision. "For we walk by faith, not by sight" (2 Cor 5.7). May we walk in the light as He is in the light (1 Jn 1.7). May His Word always be a lamp to our feet and a light to our path (Ps 119.105), for in His light we shall see light (Ps 36.9).

CHAPTER 16

Carbon – a Unique Chemical Element

Anyone who studies or just observes the natural world must be impressed by its immense variety. In outer space, here on earth, within our bodies and all around us, both the inanimate creation and the living world display variety and beauty everywhere, and thereby reflect the glory and wisdom of the Creator. Nothing that God does is ever dull or monotonous.

Just think of the millions of different substances all around us - from paper to plastics, from chalk to cheese, from wood to stone, from water to petrol, from oxygen to steel, from vitamin C to aspirin or chlorophyll … The list of materials we are familiar with is practically endless. Yet all of them are made from less than ninety different elements, primary substances into which every one could eventually be broken down. In fact most common materials are made from only about twenty elements. The commonest elements on earth are first oxygen, then silicon, aluminium and iron. The important ones for life are carbon, hydrogen, nitrogen and oxygen.

The Chemical Elements
These primary chemical elements are the basic materials from which everything is made. God designed and made each element with its own kind of atom, different from every other element, so that they could combine with each other in specific ways to produce the millions of compounds we now recognise. Thus, oxygen is an element, but combined with silicon and aluminium it makes stone, combined with calcium and carbon

it makes chalk, combined with hydrogen it is water, combined with carbon and hydrogen it makes vitamin C and aspirin, also wood and many plastics plus a huge number of other substances.

Chemistry is the science which studies the composition and properties of all materials and tries to explain why they behave in certain ways by examining their smallest particles which are called molecules. Molecules are collections of atoms bonded to each other, sometimes just a few atoms stuck together as in the case of water or carbon dioxide or methane, sometimes very large numbers of atoms as in chlorophyll or proteins or plastics (often called polymers). Molecules have different shapes and sizes and properties, and most are smaller than a millionth of a centimetre. Chemistry reveals God's handiwork at this fascinating submicroscopic level.

The different atoms which make up molecules each have their own unique substructure. Each atom contains a certain number of tinier particles called protons, neutrons and electrons. The manner in which these are arranged is another marvel, researched and discovered by scientists, even yet not completely understood, but designed and built by God. The number of electrons at the outside of an atom decides how it can make chemical bonds to its neighbouring atoms.

Atomic and molecular architecture proclaims the wisdom and glory of God. The Lord Jesus said one day, "If these should hold their peace, the stones would immediately cry out" (Lk 19.40). Every atom and molecule in the stones, or in anything else, does cry out to those who are willing to listen in an eloquent testimony to their Maker.

Carbon – the Basis of Life
Of all the elements, one is special and unique, the element carbon. It is the one from which the structures of all living things are made. Because of this, the study of carbon compounds has

traditionally been called organic chemistry. Carbon compounds are much more numerous than the compounds of any other element, and most of these are found in living things.

All living organisms are made up of compounds of carbon bonded to hydrogen, oxygen, nitrogen and less frequently, sulphur. From these few elements, all life forms have been built up and their metabolisms function. It is truly amazing that so few elements can produce such variety, and produce it in the conditions which support life. Thus in addition to smaller molecules like those of carbon dioxide, water, ammonia and amino acids, there are very large molecules, such as those of carbohydrates, proteins, fats and oils, and within each class thousands upon thousands of variations in molecular structure. It is this diverse range of substances which enables life forms to have such variety.

Carbon is the only element which can form such a wide range of different compounds. Each atom can form four bonds with atoms of other elements or with other carbon atoms, and these bonds can be single, double or triple. This opens up endless possibilities for carbon making different molecules of almost any size and three dimensional shape. The element most like carbon is silicon, but it cannot make bonds like these to any significant extent. Clearly, God designed and made the carbon atom to suit the special requirements of life.

Carbon Compounds
The processes which sustain life are very complex but also very efficient. Think, for example, of the intake and digestion of foodstuffs, repair of damaged tissue, transport of nutrients, breathing to provide oxygen which is transported in the blood producing energy for muscle action or for complex functions within cells.

For all this to happen, the substances involved need to be able to undergo changes (react) at the temperatures at which life exists. If they were too stable at those temperatures, they would not be usable, and if they were too unstable they would change too quickly before they could do their job or reach their target. It is a fascinating fact that at just the temperatures where life thrives, those very compounds of carbon possess this correct, intermediate stability. The properties of the compounds and the strength of the chemical bonds within their molecules match their usefulness at just the required temperatures – by coincidence? No, by design!

Notice how all this fits into the overall picture. Life needs a stable temperature in the 5-40 °C range. This is where
1. the relevant carbon compounds can react and change;
2. the necessary water is a liquid;
3. the earth's surface temperature lies.

We have noted already how this temperature is achieved by the sun's heating effect moderated by its distance away from us and by the effect of the atmosphere. That distance in turn has been determined by the mass of the planet. There were no afterthoughts, accidental changes, or evolving conditions to produce life. It is all one grand design put into effect by our faithful Creator for the benefit of His creatures! From the pattern of the electrons in the invisibly tiny carbon atom to the place of planet earth in the magnificently great solar system – it all reflects the manifold wisdom of God.

The Molecules of Life
Our bodies contain about 100 million million cells, most of them about two hundredths of a millimetre in size. Each cell has its own function - skin, brain, muscle, blood and so on. Each cell has a similar structure and carries all the information needed to perform many complex tasks, the most important of which is to replicate itself.

Cells can be compared to tiny computers, perfectly designed to run on biologically coded materials to produce biological results. The information is stored in the nucleus of the cell in a key substance called DNA (deoxyribonucleic acid) which stores data more efficiently and compactly than any other known system (would you expect anything else from the Creator?). It has been calculated that the information in about a million million books could be stored in a sample of DNA the size of a pinhead. The structure and function of the DNA molecule is truly astounding.

Or a cell can be compared to a miniature factory, operating according to specified rules, using efficient transporters of energy and materials, to produce certain chemical compounds. The most important of these are the proteins, synthesised from their building blocks, made exactly as the organism needs them. Millions of different molecules could be made from these raw materials, but only one will have the correct size, three dimensional shape and reactivity for its end use. The complex processes in the cell (factory) select just the one that's needed, with no unfriendly by-products and no faulty goods! The component carbon, hydrogen, oxygen and nitrogen atoms all fit together according to the design of the Creator as coded into the DNA in each cell.

Proteins do an amazing variety of jobs. They are structural tissue builders, catalysts (enzymes) for reactions, messengers and receptors of information, defenders against toxins, to mention only a few. Their molecules are all different and distinctly folded or coiled, held in place by weak bonds and by interaction with their watery environment, giving each the precise three dimensional shape which is critical to its function.

Central to all this is the unique carbon atom – a key part of the Master plan to give the world its variety and beauty, its form and function. "That it all works, and works so well, is nothing short of miraculous." [1]

---

1. From a secular textbook: *General, Organic and Biological Chemistry* by DM Feigl & JW Hill.

CHAPTER 17

Man – a Unique Being

The number of different life forms on the earth is immense. They are classified by biologists first into vegetable and animal kingdoms, then into numerous branches and types, down to individual species. The standpoint of evolution is that all of them have been derived from one common ancestor, changing over long periods of time into their present forms. The standpoint of those who believe the Bible to be the Word of God, is that all were created by Him, with differences established in the species at the beginning. Modifications ('micro-evolutions') have occurred *within established species* through selective breeding and isolation of habitat, but the long-term evolution *of new species* is an unproved theory, although a very popular one.

Of all the millions of different species, one is unique. That species is man. Man is not related biologically to any animal to which he may have a superficial resemblance, nor to any other creature or its environment even although similar chemical processes drive their metabolisms or similar fluids are found in their cells. Sharing such features is no evidence for a biological or ancestral link, although you may hear otherwise! It just means that that the Creator designed perfect and effective biochemical processes and structural units, and used them in the many living things He created, according to His own designs. This is what an architect does in designing different types of buildings, what an engineer does in producing vastly different machines. But a factory is not related to a bridge or a school, or a motor car to an aeroplane or a sewing machine!

Before we look at the many characteristics of man which are clear evidences of his unique place in creation, let us note carefully what the Bible says about the uniqueness of man.

"What is Man?"

This question is asked four times in the Bible: Job 7.17; Ps 8.4; 144.3; and Heb 2.6 (quoting Ps 8). In each case, the background is the apparent smallness or even insignificance of man in the greater scheme of things - the transience of man's troubled life in Job 7, the immense starry universe in Ps 8, the greatness and goodness of God in Ps 144. But the point of the question is the amazing thing that in man alone has God taken such a personal interest – "set Thine heart upon him", "visited him", "takest knowledge of him, makest account of him". Whilst it is evident that God cares for all His creation, man is the special object of His interest, affection, and purpose.

Man was created different. On the sixth day of creation when man was made, God said something about that act which He said about no other. The usual creative works of God were prefaced by "Let there be ..." (or equivalent), but this time we read, "Let Us make ..." (Gen 1.26-28). There was deliberate, purposeful, united activity in the Godhead. Three other special things were said: (1) "Let them have dominion ..." Man was certainly part of creation, but was given unique dominion and stewardship of it. (2) "God created man in His own image." No other creature had such dignity and such potential. (3) God "breathed into his nostrils the breath of life" (Gen 2.7). By a divine act, by the direct breath of God, man became a living soul. His body had been made of the dust of the earth, i.e., composed physically of the same chemical elements which make up the earth, just as "the earth [brought] forth the living creature after his kind" (1.24). But Adam was different, given life and a soul by the personal touch and breath of the Creator.

Man is constituted different. Man is a 'tri-partite being' consisting of "spirit, soul and body" (1Thess 5.23), resembling his Maker, the triune God, Father, Son and Holy Spirit. The *spirit* is man's highest component – it enables contact with God in a *spiritual* way (John 4.24). Man's spirit returns to God at death (Eccl 12.7). The *soul* is the real person or personality, able to be emotionally and mentally involved with people and things. The soul is immortal, living eternally in heaven or hell after death. The *body* is the physical structure which contains spirit and soul, through which we express ourselves, by which we become known to others, in which we are called to glorify God (1 Cor 6.20). At death it decomposes, to be replaced with a new body like Christ's in resurrection (Phil 3.21). The *spirit* makes us God-conscious, the *soul* makes us self-conscious, the *body* makes us world-conscious.

Man is called to be different. God made man to have real meaningful, willing communion with Him. Man made (1) "in the image of God" suggests an essential ability to represent God and display His character, and (2) "after His likeness" shows a potential ability to resemble Him and co-operate with Him. Only man has these abilities. They were seriously impaired by Adam's sin, and much of that potential was lost. But through redemption, what was lost has been restored and more besides.

There is another very important reason why God made man unique and different. The death of Christ was planned before the foundation of the world (1 Pet 1.20). To die and sacrifice Himself to bear away the sin of the world, the Son of God would become man. So man was created in such a way that God could express Himself perfectly in "flesh and blood" (Heb 2.14). The unique nature of man would fulfil what God had in mind for Himself in the incarnation of His Son as well as for man's special place in creation.

How is Man Different?
Is man just a highly developed creature, different only in degree of sophistication from "brothers" or "cousins" in the animal kingdom? In particular, has man "descended" from an ape or ape-like ancestor? No - the *evidence* is very much against this.

It is not even that man has the best of everything. For example, certain birds and animals have much more acute eyesight, hearing, and sense of smell. Indeed in terms of behaviour, man can do and has done much worse things than any other creature. Animals do not sinfully abuse their young, nor cruelly murder or sadistically torture one another, nor do they organize and make war on their own species. When predators kill, they do so for food, without hate or revenge or desire to hurt. Man is truly capable of the noblest of acts to be greatly admired, but fallen man is also capable of the most deplorable and dreadful of crimes unknown in the natural world.

As for the key differences and evidences for the uniqueness of man, here is an interesting list (more details in reference 1). Notice how totally *different* man is in so many ways from any other creature including the "primates".

Anatomically, only man has a natural *erect stance*, with *feet* and toes providing a unique base for support, whilst the *hand* is the most efficient manipulative tool available. Primates have longer thigh bones and shorter backs, naturally stooping not standing upright. Their feet are similar to their hands, designed for climbing not walking.

Mentally, only man has the ability to think deeply, to evaluate complex evidence, make difficult decisions, to be *creative and inventive*. We can do this because we are made in the image of God, and therefore we can also admire and enjoy beauty and harmony. We can compose music, make and play musical instruments, create artistic things, solve crossword puzzles and mathematical problems, understand abstract concepts of philosophy, science and justice and apply them, with a conscience to know right and wrong.

Only man can *speak, read, and write*. These amazing abilities are based upon complex systems of sounds or signs which we have to learn and be able to express. We can communicate feelings and facts, numerical and spiritual. We can laugh and cry.

Only man can make and use *tools*, some very complex and specialised – e.g., a turning lathe, a lock and key, a computer, a submarine.

For man, *work* is a meaningful activity which gives fulfilment and has objectives beyond mere survival. We do not simply work so that we can eat, or eat just to survive, as is the norm in the animal kingdom.

Only man can make, use, master and control *fire*, leading to the development of metallurgy, technology and commerce, as well as for comfort and cooking.

Only man can *organise complex systems*, whether information, materials, or whole societies (civilisations). And man can make more mess of these than any!

Human babies are much more *vulnerable and dependant* than those of any other species, with slow maturity and long development times. Family care and a safe environment for learning are important.

Man is interested in the *past and the future*, looking for answers to questions about origins and destinies, and for purpose in life. We can contemplate death. We bury our dead.

Man can *love, be faithful and true,* both to each other and to God. We can communicate with God as He can communicate with us. This is why He made us the way we are.

---

1. *Evolution or Creation*, Doorway Papers Vol 4, Part V, by A C Custance, Zondervan, 1977, www.custance.org

CHAPTER 18

Our Amazing Brain

In the course of a day we may do hundreds of things, and speak or read thousands of words. But we may think millions of thoughts. All our thoughts are generated and coordinated in a brain of truly amazing structure and complexity. Many thoughts are so fleeting that we hardly notice or remember them, others are deliberate and deep. Some bring a smile, others bring anxiety and sorrow. Some will lead to actions, others we will reject. It is our thoughts which produce our words and our deeds, for better or for worse. Therefore controlled and directed thoughts are essential for a life pleasing to God and helpful to man. So, "Think on these things," says the Bible – the things that are true, honest, just, pure, lovely, of good report, things of virtue and of praise (Phil 4.8).

When God made man in His own image, He made him body, soul and spirit. The brain is part of the body – surgeons can remove it from its protective structure (the skull), hold it in their hands, and often correct something which has gone wrong through injury or disease. But no one can lay hands upon a thought – it is not part of the body. Nor can anyone lay hands upon the mind – it too is not a physical thing. The mind is closely related to the soul, in fact sometimes in Scripture it is identified with it. The mind and soul use and direct the thoughts - intangible, unseen, but of so much potential value to God and to man. Meditations, resolves, decisions, reckonings all involve the mind and soul; in fact these shape and mould the mind and the soul, the real and significant personality, the person who is you and only you and eternally you. Meditations and resolves are very important!

Even as the hand is required for doing and the lips for speaking, so is the brain required for thinking. Just how thoughts are produced, how memories are stored and recalled, how ideas are invented and expressed is not fully known. Even how the brain controls all the functioning parts of the body, how consciously and unconsciously it keeps us going, is only partly understood. The brain by which we do understand many things has been described as beyond our understanding. It is justifiably called the most complex structure in the universe.

The Structure of the Brain
The brain has been compared to a computer, but its capacities of memory, function, speed and durability are far beyond the best ever made, *or that ever could be made*; or compared to a control centre of a busy airport, but governing a system more complex than them all put together; or to a network of information circuits hundreds of times more complex than the whole world's telephone systems - if the circuit diagram could be drawn it would cover an area of several square miles. In every respect the brain exceeds them all in complexity and efficiency.

Here are some fairly well established facts about the human brain. It is the most powerful thinking machine that can be built from the atoms in this world.
- It weighs about 1.4 kg (about 3 lbs), bigger than that of any mammal except the whale and the elephant. But in relative terms the human brain is far bigger, about 2% of body weight. The elephant's brain, about four times larger, is only about 0.1% of its body weight. This *relative* size is another feature which makes man unique in creation.
- It contains about a hundred billion neurons, each connected to about 10,000 others. A pinhead-size piece of the "grey

matter" of the brain contains around 60,000 neurons. During the development of a baby in the womb, on average 250,000 neurons are formed per minute. The neurons in one brain are more numerous than the stars in the Milky Way.

- Our brain uses about 20% of our body's energy. In other mammals this figure is 5-10%. The brain is supplied by energy and nutrients from the blood stream through an intricate system of fine blood vessels.
- The brain can process around 1 million million million information signals per second (about a hundred million times faster than any supercomputer).
- Nerve fibres convey information between brain cells. In the brain their total length is about 300,000 miles, while outside of it another 240,000 miles of nerve fibres (about one thousandth of a millimetre in thickness) carry commands and information to every part of the body. The signals are carried at about 100 mph (40 metres a second).

Brain Cells or Neurons

Each neuron is itself a marvel of complexity and function. Like all our cells it has a nucleus in which DNA is stored and used. The body of the neuron has many long streamers or dendrites (like the branches of a tree) which are spread out to reach other cells and receive impulses *from* them. It also has a longer and thicker fibre called an axon which carries impulses *to* other cells. Connection between the neurons takes place from the end of the axon of one to the dendrites of another across a narrow gap called the synapse by means of chemical signals called neurotransmitters. When a signal is thus transmitted it is like a switch being turned on. Usually a whole series of switches are turned on at once, creating a pathway among thousands of cells which is perhaps a thought pathway or a memory trace. The result of this thought may then fire off signals through nerve fibres to other parts of the body to produce action. Can you sense the wonder of all this – how a thought is produced? – and then becomes a word or a deed?

When certain skills are learned, like reading, writing, or counting, pathways are created and constantly reinforced by regular usage. When memories are recalled, pathways are again activated, but with decreasing use these may become less effective and we "can't remember". Also as we get older, some neurons may die off and usually they are not replaced. Some connections can't be made, so we forget more!

There are many types of neurons. Sensory neurons carry information from our sense organs (e.g., eyes, ears); motor neurons carry information to muscles and glands; interneurons connect between the sensory and motor neurons – they make up around 97% of the whole central nervous system. Most neurons are less than a millimetre in length, but some of the motor neurons in the spinal chord, for example, are about 1 metre long. Each has been individually designed and made for its purpose, from the shape and size of the cell right down to the electrical and chemical processes which make the connections. The whole is designed to co-operate as one brain and identify a human being. How long would all that take to evolve? It never would or could! It was created, a marvel and a miracle of God's own devising.

Sectors of the Brain
Looked at as a whole, the brain consists of two hemispheres, each of which controls the opposite side of the body. Each is covered by a 3 millimetre thick layer of nerve cells called the cerebral cortex. This is extensively convoluted (folded) to give it a large surface area. The cortex has both motor and sensory functions, and in fact different sections can be related to different abilities. For example, the sections which control and sense the hands with their intricate movements and the lips with theirs, are much bigger than those which control the neck or the hip.

The brain also contains other key organs which coordinate activity, such as the pituitary gland and the hypothalamus. The pituitary secretes hormones which are carried by the blood to other glands to stimulate their actions. The hypothalamus, the size of a pea, is an amazing control centre for eating, drinking, sleeping, body temperature and many other important automatic functions like breathing and heart beat. It also controls the pituitary.

The Mind

Beyond the brain, and yet depending on it, is the mind. The brain receives information through the senses, processes it into thoughts and memories, and the mind interprets it all in a way which influences, and is influenced by, the soul or personality of the individual.

The Scriptures often refer to the mind, and sometimes the "heart" as the seat of our emotions and desires. Thus, "as he thinketh in his heart, so is he" (Prov 23.7). "Out of the heart proceed evil thoughts ..." (Mk 7.21). "Love the Lord thy God with all thy heart and all thy soul and with all thy mind ..." (12.30). "Let this mind be in you which was also in Christ Jesus" (Phil 2.5).

How important to use our brains to think well, to focus and train our minds to love God. How necessary that we reflect the mind of Christ Jesus our Lord.

CHAPTER 19

Our Vital Blood Supply

Sometimes we pay attention to our heart beat, our pulse rate, even our blood pressure. If we get a cut or a minor injury we notice that blood flows and then it stops. At other times we are aware of our breathing getting faster after exertion and we sweat, or an indigestion pain indicates something strange happening lower down. But most of the time we do not think very much about the continuous functioning of the different parts of our bodies, unaware of how clever, complex and carefully designed they really are.

However, the more you learn about these internal organs and their functions, the more you will be amazed at just how very clever they are, and how great and wise is their Creator. When David wrote, "I will praise Thee; for I am fearfully and wonderfully made" (Ps 139.14), he had taken time to think about this. And from his very limited knowledge of it all, he did what we should do much oftener – give God the glory and the credit for it all. Lift your heart in wonder and in worship!

That wonder only becomes greater and deeper now that so much more has been discovered about anatomy, physiology, and biochemistry. Here we will sketch just a few outlines. For more details with beautiful illustrations to fascinate you, see reference 1, or look into a textbook or try an appropriate website [2]. We *are* fearfully and wonderfully made! – not evolved, not adapted, not here by chance mutations or cosmic accident! "It is He that made us and not we ourselves; be thankful unto Him and bless His name" (Ps 100.3,4).

The Heart
Our heart is a marvellously efficient pump which normally lasts for a long time, unlike other pumps which often have to be shut down for repair or maintenance. It is a hollow structure made of muscle which rhythmically contracts and relaxes around 70 times a minute, that is about 100,000 times a day, something like 2,500 million times in a normal lifetime! Four valves open and close in sequence to control the direction of the flow of blood. It weighs only about 300 grams, continuously circulating blood to enable a body weighing about 70 kg to live and function.

It has two main pumping chambers or ventricles, the right ventricle receiving blood through veins from all parts of the body where its oxygen has been depleted, and pumping it through the lungs to be reoxygenated. The left ventricle receives this oxygenated blood from the lungs and pumps it out through various arteries all through the body. The heart has its own separate blood supply without which it could not function. The coronary arteries feed blood to the heart muscles, and the coronary veins collect it in the shortest but perhaps most vital circulation loop in the body. When the heart can't get blood, its muscles can't work, and if the heart stops, we stop!

The heart responds instantly to demand for more blood from any part of the body which is working harder. The beat can go up to over 200 times per minute and also the volume of blood pumped during each heartbeat can increase. Breathing becomes much faster to supply the extra oxygen now required by the blood reaching the lungs. Oxygen enriched blood is then distributed through the arteries to reach an ever more branching system of smaller tubes and eventually into very thin walled vessels called capillaries which deliver oxygen and nutrients to cells in every part of the body. Then a similar sequence of capillaries joins up with the major veins to return the blood to the heart. The total length of our blood vessels is calculated to be about 6,000 miles, yes 6,000 miles, the distance from London to Cape Town! Stop again and say, "Marvellous are Thy works!" (Ps139.14).

Blood pumped from the heart will encounter some resistance to its flow through the branching arteries. The pressure developed can be easily measured, and safe limits for blood pressure are well recognised. If some blockage occurs in an artery or the arteries become stiffer, the effort required to push blood through will have to increase, and the heart will have to work harder. Indeed, elevated blood pressure is an indicator of arterial disease which may potentially cause heart attacks or strokes which prevent blood with its vital oxygen from reaching a key site such as the heart or the brain. It is always worth having blood pressure checked, because detection and prevention is best! God designed and gave us a marvellously functioning heart and blood circulation, and we should do our part in caring for it. Diet, exercise, lifestyle matter!

The Blood

"The life of the flesh is in the blood ..." (Lev 17.11). Written thousands of years ago, these words encapsulated the connection between blood and life long before medical and scientific research showed just how intimate and detailed that connection is. Blood is truly a marvellous fluid, performing numerous tasks which are vital to an organism.

For an adult, the volume of our blood is about 5 litres, that whole amount pumped through the heart every minute while resting. It is composed of plasma (liquid, 56%) and solid particles suspended in it (blood cells or corpuscles, 44%). There are three main types of cells – red cells, white cells, and platelets.

A drop of blood contains about 250 million red cells. Each has a lifetime of about 120 days, so they are continuously renewed (in the bone marrow) at a rate of nearly 3 million per second! Their most important function is to transport oxygen, absorbing it from the lungs and releasing it where needed. Each red cell (erythrocyte) is a wonderfully efficient unit designed for its specific purpose, from its circular disc shape which allows fast diffusion of oxygen, through to the structure of its key protein molecule called haemoglobin. Each haemoglobin molecule (made up of about 10,000 atoms) can bind four oxygen molecules to the four iron atoms in its centre in such a way that they can be reused as often as necessary without breaking any of it up. The detail of the chemistry involved is amazing, as is the whole system!

White blood cells (leucocytes) are different and much fewer. Their function is to monitor and defend the body against foreign materials and "invaders" such as bacteria, viruses and fungi. White cells recognise these invaders and in a fascinating manner, some fight against them with an array of "chemical weapons", others then actually absorb and digest them. Millions of white cells die in this process, sacrificing themselves for the benefit of the whole.

Platelets are inactive until a breach in a blood vessel is detected when they accumulate forming a plug to inhibit blood loss. These platelets can also break up to release chemical substances which promote blood clotting, just where needed to stop bleeding, but not too much or too widespread to inhibit normal circulation which would cause other serious problems. This is another amazingly effective biochemical sequence which operates continuously and even regulates its own activity according to the design of its Creator.

Every protein in this complex sequence on the molecular scale, every component of the blood on the microscopic scale, and every member of the body on the larger scale, all are necessary for the well being of the whole. Remember the important lesson from this in 1 Corinthians 12 applied to the local church? We all need each other, no member unimportant or superfluous - the hidden ones the most vital? And all must do their part - "every joint supplying, every part effectually working" (Eph 4.16).

The blood has many other important functions. It controls the body temperature at 37 °C and distributes heat throughout. It carries to all parts of the body nutrients derived from food digested in the stomach and intestines, and then processed in the liver. It also removes waste products to be filtered out in the kidneys, another amazingly efficient structure. It transports hormones, the chemical messengers of the body (e.g., adrenalin, insulin) to set in motion other processes when and where necessary. "The life of [all] the flesh *is* in the blood."

The Blood of Christ

What blood is to us physically, the precious blood of Christ is to us spiritually and eternally: without partaking of His blood by faith we have no life in us (John 6.53); without the shedding of His blood there is no remission of sins (Heb 9.22), no cleansing from sin (1 John 1.7). We are justified by His blood, (Rom 5.9); made near to God by His blood (Eph 2.13). We are in the very heart of God. What a marvel of divine purpose and a miracle of divine grace that is! Lift your heart again in wonder and worship!

---

1. *The Wonder of Man*, W Gitt, CLV Germany, 1999

2. www.kidshealth.org or www.fi.edu.org

CHAPTER 20

The Marvel of Our Birth

The development and birth of a baby is one of the most amazingly complex and wonderful things you can think of. The process of prenatal development and growth is better understood nowadays, but the marvel of it all is just as great as ever it was. Perhaps it is even greater as ultrasound scanning provides more and more fascinating information about the different stages of this development [1].

Only almighty God, the author and architect of all things, could create such a marvel. Only the Author of life could design life and give it in such a way as to be sustainable and reproducible. Theories of men have absolutely nothing acceptable to explain this. Life of any kind simply could not evolve, far less any of the highly sophisticated and marvellous forms of life which fill the world we live in, far less man with all his specialised and unique features which we have been looking at earlier. We will look at one more of these features now – birth, the climax to countless intricate, systematic, coordinated and synchronised events.

"Fearfully and Wonderfully Made"
In Psalm 139.13 -16, a beautiful description is given of the process of prenatal development, highlighting these words, "I will praise Thee, for I am fearfully and wonderfully made". In language which is poetic, yet accurate (as all Scripture is), the writer David describes how God covered (protected) him while he was "made in secret" in his mother's womb, his "members

were written in God's book", "being fashioned in continuance" before he was born, even his "unperfect substance" seen and overseen by God. Thinking about these words and the process they describe, let us look more closely at it from today's more privileged viewpoint. Here is another cause for us to marvel, more than David could, at the skill and wisdom of the One who made us, the all wise God of creation and providence, and praise Him too.

Birth is the outcome of nine months' hidden development from just two cells which unite into one at conception. This new unit then subdivides repeatedly, growing in a carefully programmed manner until everything is in place. Even by the end of the first month, the baby's nervous system and brain cells are there and growing, the tiny heart beating with its own blood supply in its own blood vessels. In the next month limbs begin to develop, every organ is in place, eyes and lips appear, even finger nails and fingerprints are forming. Everything continues to develop - internally and externally, from head to foot, from eyes and ears to airways and digestive tract and much more, to make up this amazing miracle of a baby. Add to this that the whole structure is living and mobile, that even after it is born it will go on growing for a certain number of years and then the growth will stop at the appropriate time, that most of its parts can repair themselves if broken or damaged, that each cell operates so efficiently and on such a miniature scale! It's amazing how it was all formed from two microscopic cells which fused together to become one and then to become millions upon millions of different and specialised ones. In this way God creates a dwelling place for a human soul while giving life and personality to that soul.

Now by way of comparison, think of some fine modern-day dwelling house built for someone. Think of all the foundations, walls, roofing, plumbing, windows, doors, electrical and telephone connections, heating system, ventilation, all the sophisticated equipment, the furnishings and décor and everything else. Now imagine, if you can, that it was all produced from just one basic building block! - one which somehow subdivided repeatedly to produce and fabricate the whole thing until it was complete and ready to live in! And all the information necessary to build everything correctly, and the ability to synthesise all the necessary and different building materials was also contained within this first building block which itself had been made from two separate but complementary halves! Impossible? Well, something like this but very much more happens in the formation of a baby. If you follow this rather crude comparison you might begin to grasp the marvel of birth and realise how truly beyond our comprehension is this amazing work of God! Remember Solomon's words? "As thou knowest not ... how the bones do grow in the womb of her that is with child; even so thou knowest not the works of God who maketh all" (Eccl 11.5).

Birth

During gestation, the developing baby receives all its nourishment from its mother through the placenta, an important separate structure which was formed within the first few weeks of pregnancy. The baby's blood flows into and out of the placenta where it absorbs nourishment and oxygen from the mother's blood and gets rid of waste products. The placenta also prevents the transfer of toxins and harmful substances. It is a very efficient supplier and filter and barrier, carefully designed for its purpose. It is connected to the developing baby by the umbilical cord until birth takes place when its function becomes redundant and it is discarded.

At birth an important change takes place in the baby's blood circulation. The unborn baby's lungs are unventilated, oxygen being supplied from the mother's blood as we have noted. There would be no purpose for the baby's blood going through its lungs, so these are by-passed while the blood circulates elsewhere. The by-pass is made by a special channel interconnecting the two chambers of the heart and another special duct in the pulmonary artery. At birth, as the lungs inflate, these two channels close completely and permanently and the by-pass is closed off. The normal route for the blood to circulate from the right ventricle of the heart through the lungs and into the left ventricle is ready and waiting. It is opened up and established for a lifetime, just when it is required. Amazing design, synchronism and efficiency! (more details in ref 2).

The Preciousness of Life
Over 300,000 babies are born into the world every day, each one special and unique. Sadly many babies are unwanted. Before birth many are deliberately aborted, mostly for selfish reasons, in a society which has lost direction, moral values, priorities and any sense of ultimate accountability – a consequence of evolutionary thinking. In other societies, some babies are bought and sold, and some are abandoned. But God set such a value upon each life, each soul, each baby born, that He gave His only Son to die for them.

Each child is born with a sinful nature which will all too soon become evident, and each needs to be saved from sin and its consequences. For that to be possible, our blessed Saviour had to die on a cross of suffering and shame. He said, "It is not the will of your Father which is in heaven, that one of these little ones should perish." (Matt 18.14).

Along with this we read, "Whosoever believeth in Him should not perish but have everlasting life" (Jn 3.16). So when these little ones are old enough to understand and choose, they will have to believe in Christ for themselves to be saved. But until they are mature enough to do this, if they do die perhaps due to accident or illness, they are covered safely by the sacrifice of Christ offered for sin upon the cross, and granted a place in heaven. They may die, because Adam sinned; they will live because Jesus died.

The New Birth

When our Lord Jesus spoke to Nicodemus about the necessity of being born again, he could not understand it. All he could think of was natural birth which we have been considering, and quite logically saw the impossibility of a man entering his mother's womb again to be born.

But even as children do enter a natural family by natural birth, so do individuals enter God's spiritual family by the new birth – there is no other way! The new birth is no lesser marvel and miracle than natural birth, for Nicodemus spoke for many when he said, "How can these things be?" (Jn 3.9). It could only be because God so loved the world and gave His only begotten Son (v.16).

Thus men and women can and do receive spiritual and eternal life as a gift from God by accepting and believing His Word (1 Pet 1.23) and by the working of His Holy Spirit (Jn 3.8). The new birth too is amazing. What is more, its consequences are eternal (1 Jn 3.1-2).

---

1. See for example www.nrlc.org
2. www.gynob.com/fetcirc

PART 4

CONCLUSIONS

In which we select examples from the natural world

to see more of the Creator's glory and wisdom,

to marvel at some more details of ingenious design;

and note the comparison and the contrasts

between the findings of scientific research

and the revelation of Scripture.

CHAPTER 21

Nature Study

To study nature is to study from one of God's textbooks written in glorious colour and full animation before our wondering eyes and minds! It is an ever changing but consistent display of God's handiwork, a divine art gallery, a living museum, an interactive hands-on experience which transcends any other we might encounter. It is there for us to learn from, as Scripture reminds us (1 Cor 11.14). Long ago Job gave this advice, "Ask now the beasts, and they shall teach thee; and the fowls of the air and they shall tell thee: or speak to the earth, and it shall teach thee; and the fishes of the sea shall declare unto thee." (Job 12.7 -8).

Some Lessons from Nature
Our Lord Jesus exhorted us, "Consider the ravens …God feedeth them… Consider the lilies how they grow … Solomon in all his glory was not arrayed like one of these" (Lk 12.24 -27). Consider them, not simply notice them in passing! Look at them and think about them for they teach us about *God's ceaseless care* for all His creation; and said He, "how much more" is our heavenly Father's care for us! Why are we anxious so often? Why don't we trust Him more? In the same context He called attention to the nearly worthless sparrow to remind us how detailed is this care – "even the very hairs of your head are all numbered. Fear not therefore: ye are of more value than many sparrows" (v.6-7).

The book of Proverbs draws our attention many times to insects, animals and birds. For example, "Go to the ant …; consider her

119

ways and be wise" (6.6 -8). This is a call for *our diligence and forethought*, because trusting God to provide and care for us, as He does for ravens and lilies, does not eliminate the need for us to be involved in the process of that provision! 2 Thessalonians 3.10 makes that point strongly!

In Proverbs 30, creatures as different as the horseleach, the eagle, the serpent, the lion, the greyhound have important lessons to teach. But probably best known of all in that chapter is the group of four "little but exceeding wise" things. The ants (again) teach the secret of *survival* – preparation at the right time. The conies teach the secret of *safety* – fortification in the right place. The locusts teach the secret of *strength* – congregation in the right company. The spider teaches the secret of *success* – connection for the right destination – the palace of the King! Have we learned these four secrets?

Isaiah 40.31 is an often quoted verse, for good reasons. There we read how waiting upon the Lord can have such amazing results! - to be able to "mount up with wings as eagles", how we can keep on going without fainting. Whatever the subspecies of eagle, its power in flight is its hallmark. To watch "the way of an eagle in the air" is one of the great spectacles of nature, one which Agur said was "too wonderful" for him! (Prov 30.18-19). With no apparent effort, huge wings spread out, shaped to rise on the air currents, it can climb "far far above the restless world that wars below", overcoming the force of gravity by the greater power of aerodynamics built into those magnificent wings. So we by the greater power of the indwelling Spirit of God can *rise and overcome* the forces of our old nature or circumstances which would tend to pull us down – see Romans 8.2.

Variety in Nature
Beauty, variety and harmony mark all the works of God. For all the millions of species in the vegetable and animal kingdoms, each has its own characteristics to enable us to recognise it. Each

has its own place in the ecological system, from the invisibly small to the amazingly large - from the tiniest insects to the great quadrupeds of Africa, from the minute plankton to the great sea mammals of the Southern Ocean, from the miniature lichens and mosses to the giant redwood trees of North America. How beautifully everything blends together! No clashing, jarring colours, no awkward shapes, no grotesque features. It is one harmonious whole, individual parts of it breathtakingly beautiful! God made it "pleasant to the sight" (Gen 2.9) and so we find it. The God who delights in beauty has given this sense to us also. That is why we can really enjoy and appreciate beauty and harmony as no other creature can.

Knowing the characteristics of different creatures is important to us for another reason. *Nature study helps our Bible study!* We won't grasp the full meaning of Scripture references to different birds, beasts, flowers, insects and so on, unless we know something about them. For example, if we did not know about certain animals, we would miss the full significance of those titles of our Lord Jesus, "Lamb of God" and "Lion of the tribe of Judah" (Rev 5). If we do not know something about the different beauties of flowers we will not grasp the difference between "the Rose of Sharon" and the "Lily of the Valley" (Song 2.1) and might miss something about the beauty of the Lord Jesus. We can see the depth of His concern for Jerusalem when we watch the hen gathering her brood under her wings, and similarly understand better His assessment of Herod as "that fox" (Luke 13.34,32) when we know what kind of animal that is. Lessons about clean and unclean creatures will be easier to apply to ourselves if we know something about those different animals, birds, fishes and insects which are listed in Leviticus 11.

Nature Poems
If nature is a subject worth studying, it must also be one worth writing about, and writing poetry about. Of all the thousands of 'nature poems' two of the most beautiful ones are found in

the Bible. Like most good poems, they are there to stir emotions and admiration.

Take *Psalm 104* to begin with. It exhorts us, beginning and end, to "Bless the Lord". Its partner Psalm 103 does the same. In that Psalm we bless His holy name as our Redeemer because of His mercy and grace towards us. In this one we bless Him as our Creator because of His work and wisdom all around us. Survey again His "very great" skill laying the foundations (v.1 -9); admire the provision of essential water to nourish beast and bird, to produce food and beauty (v.10 -15); take the tour through the trees, the seasons and the seas (v.16 -26); note the cycle of life and death at the command of God (v.27- 33); say with the poet, "O Lord, how manifold are Thy works... My meditation of Him shall be sweet: I will be glad in the Lord" (v.24, 34).

Or go now to *Job 38 - 41*. This is God's own great poem, stirring, awe-inspiring words spoken to His suffering servant Job after many chapters of "words without knowledge" (38.2). This is now pointed, precise, meaningful. God asks Job a total of eighty questions about the natural world in its great variety. He moves in a gigantic panorama from the skill and power which created everything on to His control of the sea, the snow, the stars, to the life cycles of beasts and birds, on to mighty behemoth on the land and invincible leviathan in the sea [1]. It is a revelation of a God who creates and a LORD who cares. What a poem it is! The sheer magnificence of it all leaves Job speechless, bowed in humility before God. He can no more comprehend all of this than he can comprehend how the God He served so well had tested him to the limit. He could not see behind his circumstances, nor can we, but God is always in control! That is one of nature's great lessons.

---

1. Behemoth and leviathan may well be different dinosaurs – the descriptions fit them better than any other known creatures.

CHAPTER 22

Design and Instinct

Detailed studies of many creatures have revealed just how beautifully they fit into their place in the natural world. It is not that they have evolved by 'chance mutations' and by adapting to their environment, with one species eventually changing into another. They were designed and made to be what they are and where they are. In a given species, adaptation to surroundings does produce changes in some of their characteristics, for example brown bears in the forests and polar bears in the Arctic, but new species are not formed that way.

However, such detailed studies on living things have not explained everything about them, indeed some of the most fascinating aspects remain the least understood. To illustrate this, let us consider the birds again, beautiful, interesting creatures, common everywhere in their great variety. Both what is understood and what is not understood about them point repeatedly to the wisdom and provision of almighty God.

Birds and Flying

Made by God on the fifth day of creation week (Gen 1.20), their obvious characteristics are their wings for flying and their reproduction of young by laying eggs. If female birds were to carry their young until birth, as many other mammals do, think how their ability to fly would be seriously impaired and their survival jeopardised. See how this and the other characteristic features we examine next, demonstrate God's integrated design for birds and no other type of creature.

The *wing of a bird* fulfils aerodynamic design requirements, both for flapping and for gliding – it did this long before that word was thought of! Each flight feather is also cleverly designed: the central hollow shaft and the side 'barbs' with smaller 'barbules' zipping together give the lightest, strongest structure for a wing. Could this marvellous structure evolve from the scales of a reptile? In addition, feathers provide insulation and camouflage in hazardous habitats.

The *bones of birds* are hollow and cross braced inside. Engineers tell us that this type of structure gives maximum strength with minimum weight – just what birds need! A special example is 'shock absorber' bones in the skull of a woodpecker which prevent damage to its head while like 'a flying power drill' it repeatedly slams its sharp beak into solid wood.

Birds' lungs are basically different from those of other creatures. We breathe air in and out from the top of our lungs, but in birds the air flows in at the top and out at the bottom of their lungs while their blood flows through in the opposite direction. This gives a much better absorption of oxygen. So birds can fly fast and far, and many fly at high altitudes where reduced oxygen levels are a severe handicap for man and beast. This is amazing – but not surprising when we see it as God's design!

Some birds fly very fast. The peregrine falcon is the fastest creature in the world, able to swoop on its prey at around 180 mph. Other birds fly very far. The arctic tern which you can see around the north Scottish coasts each summer holds the record. It flies over 10,000 miles north from the Antarctic every springtime and returns south again the same distance every autumn. During its lifetime this beautiful bird flies the same distance as a trip from the earth to the moon and back!

Migration
Spring and autumn migration is a fascinating thing. In their millions, arctic and other terns, flocks of swallows, swifts and

martins, and thousands of other types of birds worldwide, make such journeys. Every April, the arrival of the osprey in Scotland from Africa is eagerly awaited, coming back to its old nest site to breed. And there are few experiences to rival the sight and sound of skeins of geese spread across a clear autumn sky, these stretched out V formations of perhaps a thousand birds at a time, calling loudly to announce their presence, arriving from the Arctic circle to spend the winter here.

How all these migrant birds navigate over such vast distances and find their way repeatedly to exactly the same spot year on year, is an unsolved puzzle! Particularly astonishing is how young birds find their way for the first time, when maybe weeks earlier their parents have gone away without them. Instinct is the name given to it, but no one knows what the mechanism is – only God, for He put it there.

The instinct of birds like these is set as a challenge to us in Psalm 84.3. How much of a 'homing instinct' do we have for the presence of God, for His house, His altars? Whether travelling far like the swallow or staying local like the sparrow, do we always seek out our spiritual home and feel we belong there? Is that where we want to be again and again?

Migration is not confined to birds. Salmon born in an upland river bed make their way downstream to the open sea where they mature and grow. They may spend up to four years in the ocean far from the river of their birth. Then they return to that selfsame section of the very river where they were born, leaping up raging waterfalls, overcoming huge obstacles, to lay their eggs in those gravel beds for the next generation to repeat all over again, a wonderful cycle of nature. Perhaps the largest migration spectacle in the world is seen in the Serengeti grasslands of central Africa when annually around two million wildebeest migrate huge distances, crossing wide rivers full of hungry crocodiles, and then return some months later.

Other Puzzles

Hibernation is another unusual thing. Certain animals like the hedgehog, the bat, and some types of squirrel go into a deep sleep for the winter months and then wake up in the spring. During this time their body temperature drops to conserve energy. But how do they stay alive without feeding for so long? How do they know when to fall asleep and wake up? Some females even carry young during hibernation and give birth shortly after waking up!

How do bats see in the dark as they dart about, catching insects on the wing? How do they avoid colliding with each other and with any obstacles? They actually have an inbuilt 'radar' or 'echolocation' system. They emit short pulses of high frequency sound and receive echoes back to their ears with such precise detail that they are able to locate food supplies and 'fly blind', without interference from the echoes from the other bats all around. They actually 'see' in the dark by hearing!

There are many other fascinating, unexplained puzzles in all of nature. How does a beautiful butterfly or moth develop from a crawling caterpillar through a hard chrysalis? How does a chameleon's automatic camouflage system work? What is the strange 'dance of the bee' which communicates precise information to the rest of the swarm about food supplies? Why do certain animals bond closely with humans but others don't?

And it's not only in the animal kingdom that such questions arise. What about plants and trees? Why and how do deciduous trees lose their leaves in autumn, treating us to such a rich palette of glorious changing colours, then clothe themselves again in every shade of green each springtime, whilst the evergreens keep their colour all year round and often treat us to the silent beauty of their branches crusted with frost or laden with snow on a hard winter's day?

No one knows the complete answer to such questions. You may be told that scientists have discovered that it is due to the response of enzymes to conditions like light or temperature, or that in the case of animals it has to do with food supplies or suitable breeding habitat, and this is true. But how do they all know when and how to do it and where to go? And where did these regulating enzymes and intricate mechanisms come from? As in most branches of science, the more we discover, the more we find out what we do not know! There are more questions than answers!

Ecclesiastes 3.11 tells us this: "He hath made everything beautiful in his time ... [yet] no man can find out the work that God maketh from the beginning to the end." But the beauty of it is ours to enjoy, the wonder of it ours to appreciate. In all of nature, in all the universe, design is to be found everywhere. It certainly is "intelligent design", but it is more than that - it is ingenious, awesome! It all points us to its great Creator. Both the beauty of the discovered details and the marvel of the unsolved puzzles call us to worship Him!

"Whatsoever God doeth, ... nothing can be put to it, nor anything taken from it: and God doeth it, that men should fear before Him." (v.14).

CHAPTER 23

Science and Scripture

At the beginning of this book on creation, we started from the position that "the foundation of the Lord stands sure, His Word is totally trustworthy, and a belief in the literal Bible account of origins is totally sustainable". This position has been well justified by examining widely and in depth many examples of the design and efficiency which pervade the natural world all around us and the physiological processes deep within us. In this final chapter, we will consider something of the broader relationship between science and the Scriptures. Our thesis is that they complement each other. They are not in disagreement. In fact, it has been shown repeatedly that science supports the revelation of Scripture [1].

Science

The pursuit of science is now almost 400 years old. Its beginnings were slow and modest, but in this 21st century it has a major influence upon every aspect of our daily lives and is an essential component of education and civilisation everywhere. Many of its results and applications have undeniably improved our health and material well being.

But what is science? The word means 'knowledge', and that is the sense in which it is used in 1 Timothy 6.20. In the first century there was no 'science' in the presently accepted sense, but there were threats from a 'knowledge system' which rejected God. Such systems and their threats change their form throughout history, but they are as old as time (see Gen 3.1-5) and as modern as today.

Science nowadays is defined as *an organised and correlated body of knowledge about the material world which is based upon observation and measurement, and developed by experiment and thought.* Science attempts to understand the workings of the natural world and to simplify or unify the laws by which it operates, often using quite elegant mathematics to do so. This makes it rather mysterious and daunting to many people. The danger in this is that what scientists say and propose is often simply accepted uncritically. It can be difficult to distinguish the established facts and basic laws of science from the proposals and theories which may be propagated for reasons beyond the actual limits of science. Evolution theory is a prime example of this – an ideological necessity for some whose drive is atheism.

Science does have its limits. It is limited to **the material world,** 'matter' as it is called, and it can deal only with **what can be measured** (in terms of the three fundamental quantities of mass, length and time). From such measurements, laws and theories are developed, then predictions can be made of what is not directly measurable. This is called extrapolation. We have noticed before that such extrapolations sometimes lead to erroneous conclusions especially when the conditions are very far removed from the experimental ones. Such conclusions can only be accepted when they are tested and verified by new experimental evidence.

From this at least two points are worth repeating. First, those statements you hear about such things as the origin of the universe, the age of the earth, the origin and development of life, are all based upon huge extrapolations which because of their very nature cannot be tested by experiment. They are therefore not scientific facts. They are simply the popular ideas of those who either follow the dogma of the majority opinion or do not wish to believe otherwise. Second, because God is a spirit, science is totally unable to say anything about Him – He cannot be measured, cannot be proved or disproved by science. No one can find God through science alone (Job 11.7). God is found through faith (Heb11.6).

Science tries to simplify things by using the principle of 'reductionism' - reducing systems to their simplest components for study and explanation. So science will attempt to explain everything in nature in terms of its material components, its matter only. But there are many things which we encounter in life which are not material things and cannot be measured or explained in terms of matter only. For example, the emotions of love and hate, the appreciation of beauty and wonder - these are not material things. Neither is the spiritual dimension to life which Christians have found to be no less real than the material or natural, indeed we believe it is much more important. By definition it is super-natural.

Information
Something else is found throughout the natural world which is not a material thing. It is information, and information is very important. It exists everywhere, but especially in living things which require matter and energy *and information* to be able to function. The storage and transfer of information uses material things as in the books we read, the barcodes we scan, the DNA in every cell, hormones in the blood stream, and so on. But the information these things contain and transmit is something beyond the material symbols or code. It has to do with intelligence and ability to communicate. Information is not matter and cannot be reduced to it. Information is a fundamental entity in nature, different from and as important as the other fundamentals of energy and matter [2].

The laws of information science, now very relevant in this digital age, state that information requires a source, a receptor, and a transmitting code. Information never arises of itself, never comes from nothing or nowhere. Also codes which transfer information never arise by chance, they always require intelligent design. The source of all information in the universe is the One who is wisdom itself (Prov 8.12-31).

The most valuable information of all has been given in the Holy Scriptures – this revelation from God (2 Tim 3.16) of which we can be receptors. It has been transferred and communicated to us not in a strange code but in a way we can understand, by holy men of God speaking (writing) by the Holy Spirit (2 Pet 1.21). The overall purpose of it all is that we might be made wise unto salvation through faith which is in Christ Jesus. That is far more important than discovering distant worlds in space or microscopic details of creatures nearby. These are interesting things which do indeed declare the glory of God, but they are not of ultimate importance.

To create them all, God spoke and it was done, He commanded and it stood fast (Ps 33.9), an amazing work of power! But to save us from our sins and bring us to Himself in a righteous relationship of grace, He "sent His only begotten Son into the world that we might live through Him" (1 Jn 4.9), an amazing work of love! This is the ultimate and the best. Creation cannot teach it, but the Scriptures teach it clearly! No other message is better, no results are greater, nothing more wonderful than this glorious gospel! We who have received this information, this eternal truth, must transmit it to others. Let us make sure that we do transmit it in a way which those others can understand, not in some strange coded language peculiar to ourselves.

Conclusion

Science deals with observed facts about material things, then deduces and theorises, appealing to our intellect. The Bible deals with spiritual needs and values, and calls for our faith. It was not written to teach science, but something more important and personal and lasting. Although such an ancient book, it contains no ancient absurdities or anything which is incompatible with validated modern science. The Book of Nature and the Book of

Scripture should be studied side by side. No disagreements or contradictions will be found, because God is the author of both.

To find out the truth is important. Sadly some people cannot be bothered to do this, some even believe that there is no such thing as truth, just opinions and relative values, and they drift on through life without any fixed reference point or purpose. Others actively pursue knowledge by research, seeking answers by means of measurement, intellect and reason. Many amazing things about the material world have been discovered in this way.

But answers to deeper and more relevant questions, questions about spiritual values, about origins and destinies, about our relationships with God and with man, are not to be found by that type of research. They lie outside the scope and limits of science. They are found rather in the revelation which God has so graciously given in the Bible and in the person of Christ Jesus His beloved Son. Divine revelation transcends all human research. It is permanent, indeed eternal, and totally trustworthy.

-----

1. "As I hope the evidence presented in this book has shown, science, which has been for centuries the great ally of atheism and scepticism, has become at last, in these final days of the second millennium, what Newton and many of its early advocates had so fervently wished – 'the defender of the anthropocentric faith'." Michael Denton, *Nature's Destiny*, the Free Press New York, 1998, p.389.
2. See W Gitt, *In the Beginning was Information*, CLV Germany, 2000.

Glossary and Reference Material

Atom
The smallest particle of an element, composed mainly of protons, neutrons and electrons held together by special short range forces.

Chemical elements
The simplest forms of matter into which every substance can eventually be decomposed. About ninety of these are found on earth, ranging from hydrogen to uranium. The commonest is oxygen.

DNA
Deoxyribonucleic acid, the long chain spiral polymer which holds the genetic information of every living cell.

Einstein's Equation
Gives the relationship between mass (m) and energy (E), showing how much energy can theoretically be obtained from a certain mass of matter, e.g., in a nuclear reaction. It is $E = mc^2$ where c is speed of light (below).

Electromagnetic waves
The form of radiation which passes through space from different sources, ranging in a huge spectrum from radio waves with long wavelengths (several km) to X rays with very short wavelengths. The light which our eyes can see is a very small section of this spectrum. All types of this radiation travel at the same speed – the speed of light (see below).

Enzyme
A complex protein which promotes a reaction or change within a living system at the molecular level – a "living catalyst".

Extrapolation
A method in science which uses a relationship found to be true in certain limited conditions and applies it to much different conditions where it has not been tested. There is no guarantee that it will be true under the new conditions – other laws may interfere.

Light year
The distance which light travels in a year's time, calculated to be 9.46 million million km (or 5.88 million million miles); found by multiplying speed of light (given below) by the number of seconds in a year.

Molecule
The smallest particle of a compound, made up of atoms bonded to each other.

Speed of light
The fastest known speed in the universe of 299,792.5 km per second (or 186,398 miles per second). At this speed, light from the sun, about 93 million miles away, takes a bit over 8 minutes to reach the earth.

Bibliography

The following list is a limited and personal selection of some of the books which the author has found helpful and useful, some over many years. It is not a comprehensive list.

Abou-Rahme, Farid. *And God Said;* 135 pages. John Ritchie Ltd, Kilmarnock, 1997.
Easy to read on "Science and the Bible"; much about Creation and the Flood; scriptural and evangelical.

Ashton, John F (Ed). *In Six Days: why fifty scientists choose to believe in creation;* 384 pages. Master Books, Inc, USA, 2001.
Personal testimonies of practising scientists in several disciplines; includes some in-depth analysis of evidence.

Blanchard, John. *Has Science got rid of God?;*160 pages. Evangelical Press, 2004.
Clearly written, convincing and well presented like the rest of this author's longer and shorter "apologetic" works.

Custance, Arthur C. *Evolution or Creation.* Doorway Papers Vol 4; Zondervan, 1977. [www.custance.org].
A detailed study of the pointers from many branches of science to creation. (Adopts an "old earth" viewpoint.)

*Davies, Paul. *The Goldilocks Enigma,* 349 pages. Allen Lane, 2006.
An exploration by a modern physicist of how the universe is "just right" for life.

*Denton, Michael J. *Nature's Destiny: How the laws of Biology reveal Purpose in the Universe;* 454 pages. The Free Press, New York, 1998.
Interesting and thoroughly detailed treatment of many aspects of nature by a secular biologist showing how the creation of man is central to the universe. Similar to his earlier book, Evolution: a Theory in Crisis.

Gitt, Werner. *In the Beginning was Information*; 256 pages. Christliche Literatur-Verbreitung (CLV) Bielefeld, Germany, 2nd English edition 2000.
Very useful and interesting discussion of Information Science, how it necessitates a Creator, and applies to the message of the Bible.

Gitt, Werner. *Stars and their Purpose*; 217 pages. Christliche Literatur-Verbreitung (CLV) Bielefeld, Germany, 2nd English edition 2000.
A fascinating study of astronomy and its pointers to the Creator - thoroughly evangelical.

Gitt, Werner. *The Wonder of Man*; 155 pages. Christliche Literatur-Verbreitung (CLV) Bielefeld, Germany, 1st English edition 1999.
A beautifully illustrated treatise on the special and complex nature of man's anatomy, and a challenging section about man's need of salvation.

Meldau, Fred J. *Why we believe in Creation not in Evolution*; 348 pages. Christian Victory Publishing Co, Denver, USA, 1959.
A treasure trove of many interesting observations throughout the natural world which proclaim creation and defy evolution, older but still useful material.

Morris, Henry M and Whitcomb, John C. *The Genesis Flood: the Biblical Record and its Scientific Implications*; 518 pages. Baker Book House, Michigan, 1975 (first published 1961).
A thorough examination of key aspects of creationism as supported by scientific findings especially in geology – a classic in this field.

*Penrose, Roger. *Shadows of the Mind*; 457 pages. Vintage, 1995.
A mathematical examination of the workings of the mind – concluding from very detailed evidence that the mind cannot be explained in terms of science, and that understanding is not a computational quality. Understanding is not man-made!

*These authors profess no commitment to belief in God, but the conclusions they reach from their scientific work are remarkable.

Index

Creation's Story